Rosella Vantaggi

SIENA
city of art

Publication authorised by

CONSORZIO PER LA TUTELA DEL PALIO DI SIENA

Distributed by
FABIO TURBANTI
Via B. Tolomei 9 - Tel. 0577-51260
SIENA

CENTRO STAMPA EDITORIALE

PERSEUS

Index

Siena, city of art

The tourist who goes along the modern road leading to Siena from Florence, sees all around himself a very pleasant landscape, rich in green fields of olive-trees, vineyards and cypresses. The medieval and characteristic towers of S. Gimignano rising on the right side, near Poggibonsi, tell us that Siena is near. The landscape looks quite different to those who reach the town through the south of the province by the Cassia or Valdichiana roads. This side of the country, though bare in some of its parts, presents characteristic and suggestive features, thanks mainly to its picturesque clays and hills of clay with their corn-fields. On top of these hills there is always a tree, as if it were a sort of plume.

Siena was a Roman colony during the Republican age. During the imperial age and the early Middle Ages, it went through many terrible events. Its expansion, however, was always limited by the greater power and rivalry of Florence. Being far from the sea and open only towards the lands of the Maremma, Siena was often besieged and devastated and had to face civil wars and terrible pestilences.

After the domination of the Longobards and Franks, it passed under the Bishop-Counts, towards the middle of the 11th century. Then there was the turn of the Consuls, with a lay government. And it was in this period that Siena reached the height of its political and economic power, especially after the famous battle of Montaperti in 1260, by which it defeated the Florentines. Arts and culture flourished in this time. Thanks mainly to the Government of the Nine, which, restored in 1277, ruled for about 70 years, the magnificent monuments of Siena were built during this period of time. The renowned "Piazza del Campo" is its most precious pearl and the centre of its peculiar town-planning. This square, with its famous buildings, is the spacious and resounding shell, where the city-life takes place. It is the suggestive amphitheatre, whose background is constituted only by the "Palazzo Pubblico" with the Tower of Mangia, the best example of 14th century civil architecture. The characteristic medieval look of Siena dates back to the same century. The town has kept its original look. In its streets made of bricks and stones, among the high buildings, adorned with elegant three-mullioned windows and slender ogive arches, in the suggestive

THE "MAESTÀ", fresco by Simone Martini, detail.

courtyards, in the closed and dark entrance halls, in the narrow alleys and squares, you perceive a sort of ancient atmosphere, which makes Siena so charming.

It is a medieval town, but mostly a town of art. If one is intensely excited at the sight of the Campo, one is amazed at the sight of the monuments of the town, the Cathedral and the other churches, the museums. Everywhere one finds precious masterpieces, wonderful works by Nicola and Giovanni Pisano, Duccio and Simone Martini, Donatello and Ghiberti, who have left here some examples of their immortal art.

Painting, which was the most genuine and significant expression of the creativeness of the Sienese, new architectonic ideas and an original school of sculpture, one of the best in Italy, more refined techniques in gold working and designs, made of Siena one of the

greatest leaders in the field of art in Italy and Europe, since the end of the 13th century and the early 14th century. If in the 14th century Sienese art reached its height with Duccio and Simone Martini, Pietro and Ambrogio Lorenzetti, we must not forget that during the two next centuries the figurative arts reached very high levels, thanks to artists like Jacopo della Quercia, Sassetta, Sano di Pietro, Giovanni di Paolo, just to mention a few. When in the 17th century the Town of Siena declined because of internal divisions and the decreasing richness of its merchants and bankers and so was overcome by the rising power of Florence and annexed to the Grand Duchy of Tuscany, its people took refuge, as it were, in the glories of the past, in its institutions and greatest memories.

Being conscious of having a personality of their own, the Sienese people kept their love for the old

districts, their civil and religious traditions, the Palio, which is something more than a horse-race. The Palio is a wonderful show commemorating the glory of the ancient Republic. It is a popular feast, which, since the Middle Ages, aroused people's enthusiasm. By the Palio, the Sienese express the feelings and passions of their 17 "contrade" or districts. And it is by this fight among the contrade that the ancient Siena goes on living together with the actual Siena, in the harmonious and suggestive atmosphere of an historical and artistic environment, which is unique in the world.

Piazza del Campo

Piazza del Campo on a pleasant Spring morning: the shadows of the Palazzo Pubblico and the Tower of Mangia on the square and the nearby buildings suggestively reproduce the silhouette of the most famous Sienese building. It is famous because it is beautiful and represents the architectonic unity of the square. This building, however, is not connected with the square only from the artistic, but also historical, traditional and cultural points of view. It was here that the Sienese, through the centuries, have faced the most important events of their history; it was here that they have rejoiced and suffered. If the Campo is the heart of Siena, the backdrop of its past history and centre of its life, the Palazzo is the symbol of that history, the guardian of its dearest memories and cultural values. The noblest feelings of the people of Siena go on living in this square, which is the most important testimony of the extraordinary artistic and cultural development during the age of the Free Towns.

Palazzo Pubblico, Cappella di Piazza and Torre del Mangia

The peculiar shape of Piazza del Campo or simply "il Campo" (the Field) is due to the canalization and diversion of rain-waters on an irregular and bare ground, shaped like an amphitheatre, where the three hills, on which Siena rises, meet together. This happened during the 13th century. This square, however, is incomparably beautiful and the essential element of Sienese town-planning. It is famous all over the world and unique of its kind. It looks like a shell, which shows the particular nature of the ground, harmonizing nature and art. It is paved along its borders, while the central part is made of bricks arranged like a fish-bone and divided into nine parts by white stone-strips, which commemorate the Rule of the Nine. At the base of the shell, as a sort of background on the wide cavea of the square, is the Palazzo Pubblico (Public Palace), surrounded by remarkable buildings, with the slender Tower of Mangia. and, at its foot, the Cappella di Piazza (the chapel of the

Square). It is magnificent and elegant, simple and picturesque at the same time, in its structure and harmonious division of its area. It is the most renowned of the Gothic-Tuscan buildings and the best example of Sienese civil architecture, which, more than others, presents more slender lines and a peculiar ornate style.

The history of this building is strictly connected with the political and economic affairs of Siena. It was begun in 1250 as records of that time show. In 1299 the central part was completed, while the building of the two wings was begun in 1305. In 1310 the Palazzo had the shape which it kept till in 1680 and at the beginning of the 18th Century some other parts were added to its structure, though the stylistic unity of its front was kept. The front is made of stone in its lower part with the characteristic Sienese arches. The second and third storeys are made of bricks, with

Palazzo Pubblico.

two orders of three-mullioned windows. A fourth storey, higher than the two side bodies, with small arches and merlons. Among the mullioned windows of this storey there is a large copper disk with the monogram of Christ, the symbol of St. Bernardine, and on the sides two stone she-wolves. The Palazzo Pubblico was once the seat of the Government and the Mayor of the ancient Sienese Republic. Today it is the seat of the Municipality.

Cappella di Piazza surmounted by the Tower of Mangia, was built to fulfill a vow made by the Sienese during the 1348 pestilence. It was begun in 1352 by Domenico d'Agostino and completed around 1376 by Giovanni di Cecco who completed also the pillars and the roof.

The Tower of Mangia, this slender tower, dominating the town, shows not only the architectonic genius of the workers of that time but is also a great work of engineering. It is called so after Giovanni di Duccio, named "Mangiaguadagni" o more simply "Mangia", engaged by the Municipality to ring the bells. The automaton, which was put there to strike the hours on the tower till 1780, was called "Mangia". The brick pipe was erected by the Aretine brothers Minuccio di Rinaldo and Francesco Naldi, under the direction of Giovanni d'Agostino (1338-1348).

After a very slender cornice, there is the first travertine coping, with two coats-of-arms of the Municipality, with a rampant lion in the middle, then the bell-tower made to designs by Lippo Memmi (1341). Above it there is the big bell cast in 1665 and called by the Sienese "Campanone" or "Sunto", because it was "christened" Maria Assunta.

Palazzo Pubblico - a detail of the facade, with the flags of the 17 "contrade" of Siena during the Palio.

15

Palazzo Pubblico: The Mayoris Courtyard

One reaches it by a door near the Cappella di Piazza. It was built in 1325 and restored in 1929. It consists of a portico surmounted by a storey with a series of large three-mullioned windows. Along the walls there are some coats-of-arms of Mayors and a fresco, badly damaged and incomplete, dating back to the 14th century and representing the Madonna and two angels. In the photo: the remains of the statue of "Mangia" and "The She-wolf feeding the twins", a golden tin work by Giovanni di Turino (1429-30), which are in the vestibule and at the end of the portico.

Right: Cappella di Piazza.

Palazzo Pubblico: The Sala del Mappamondo

The large council hall known as the Sala del Mappamondo (from a map painted by Ambrogio Lorenzetti in the 14th century and now lost) is situated on the first floor of the Palazzo Pubblico, whose rooms are now laid out as a Civic Museum. On the end walls are the two great frescoes of the Maestà and Guidoriccio da Fogliano by Simone Martini. This latter fresco, as we will explain below, has become the Symbol of the civil and military power of the glorious Republic of Siena. In recent years, during a restoration carried out under the direction of the Superintendent of Artistic and Cultural Properties Piero Torriti, another significant fresco came to light

in its lower part: it depicts a Castle and a Church with two personages in the foreground; undoubtedly antecedent in date to Simone Martini's fresco, it has plausibly been attributed to Duccio di Buoninsegna (c. 1314-15). Below, a view of the hall with the "Maestà" in the background. This is the first work which can be securely attributed to Simone Martini. This artist was one of the greatest representatives of 14th century painting. If, according to Vasari, he died in 1344, when he was 60, it means that he was born in 1284. Simone painted the "Maestà" in 1315. Six years after, however, he had to restore the fresco because it was damaged by damp. Under a canopy supported by eight apostles, the Madonna and Child enthroned are surrounded by angels, saints and other apostles. A wide strip of 20 medallions with images of Christ, prophets and evangelists surrounds the composition. Below, in the centre, we see a double-faced figure representing the old and new laws and a medallion reproducing the seal of the Republic.

Guidoriccio da Fogliano, fresco by Simone Martini

On the opposite side, above, there is another fresco by Simone Martini, representing "Guidoriccio da Fogliano" after the victory over the Castles of Montemassi and Sassoforte of Maremma, which had rebelled in Siena in 1328. The work, completed in 1329, was a part of a series of representations of Castles conquered by the Sienese Republic. Unfortunately this work has been lost. In the centre, the "condottiero" (leader), magnificently paraded, proud and silent, triumphantly going towards the conquered castles. This fresco is certainly one of the best and most famous works of Simone Martini. The vast scene presents a sort of monumental magnificence, with the towered castles in the background. It is really a poetic and heroic evocation of the event.

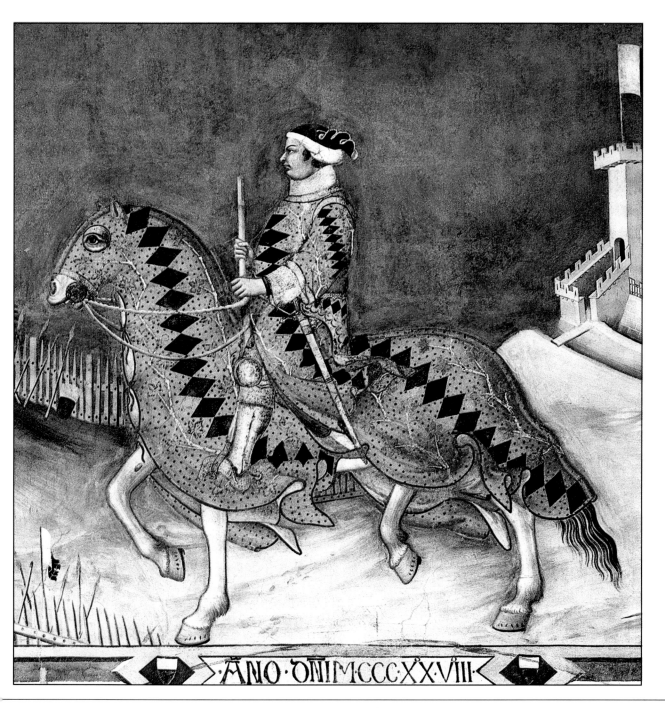

The Maestà, fresco by Simone Martini

I t is considered the oldest fresco of all Sienese painting. In this work Simone Martini combines the refined "French Gothic" style with Hellenistic elements taken from Duccio and new elements of Italian art, represented by the Pisan sculptors and Giotto. The intense expressions of the characters, the delicate lines, the vivid colours, the refined details, all take you into another mystical reality.

THE "MAESTÀ", by Simone Martini
(after the restoration).

Sala della Pace or Sala dei Nove: Allegory of Good Government and Effects of Bad Government

This hall is so called because it was the seat of the Government of the Nine. In it is kept the most famous cycle of secular frescoes of all Sienese painting. It is one of the works of Ambrogio Lorenzetti of Siena (1319-1348) painted between 1337 and 1339.

The great political, didactic and moral representation consists of three parts: "The Allegory of Good Government", which can be seen in the photo above; "The Results of Good Government in the town and countryside", and "The Allegory and the Results of Bad Government", below, all forming one composition. Unfortunately the latter one is badly damaged.

"The Good Government" is represented by an old, solemn king dressed in white and black. These are the colours of the "Balzana", the Sienese flag, and the coat-of-arms of the town. On his left side, Justice, Temperance and Magnanimity; on his right side, Prudence, Fortitude and Peace. Above, the three theological virtues, while at the feet of the King the She-wolf feeds Aschius and Senius, sons of Remus and mythical founders of Siena. Below, "The Results of Good Government in the town" (a detail): a view of 14th century Siena where, among towers and embattled buildings, various activities flourish, with elegant cavalcades along its streets, young dancers crowding the squares and streets of the town. Here are the harmoniously combined features of a society, which is happy thanks to the great virtues of the "Good Government".

Detail of the Good Government.

Another detail of the Results of Good Government: a door in the city walls opens on to the countryside, where life pulses among farm-houses, castles, vineyards, woods and olive-groves. In the side picture: the dancers.

This is the most lively and interesting composition of the whole cycle. Lorenzetti describes here everyday life - the market, a cavalcade outside the gates, a lady dressed in red on a white horse, dancing girls. Each event, however, and each figure bear witness to the 14th century way of life and its deep and genuine values. It is so that the imposing conceptual and allegorical structure, based on the contrast between good and evil, good and bad government, becomes poetry by a very original language.

And it is in this work that Ambrogio Lorenzetti reached his artistic ideal, which expresses itself in the perfect balance of all the values, between colour and volume, in the lines clearly marking mass and colour.

Detail of the Good Government.

Chapel of the Palazzo Pubblico, the Choir

Near the Globe Hall there is a magnificent chapel, closed by an elegant wrought-iron gate, designed probably by Jacopo della Quercia and made in 1437 by the Sienese Giacomo di Vita and his son Giovanni. Above the marble altar by Marrina, there is a beautiful painting by Sodoma representing the "Holy Family and St. Leonard". On the vaults of the walls of the chapel there are frescoes made by Taddeo di Bartolo around 1407 and representing the Evangelists, the Doctors of the Church, various prophets and stories of the Virgin's life. Below, the funeral of the Madonna.

Along the walls of the chapel one can admire a precious wooden choir with 21 stalls, all carved, with carved panels on their backs, illustrating the articles of the Creed. It is one of the works of Domenico di Niccolò, who, having made this choir, was called "Domenico dei Cori". This choir, made between 1415 and 1428, is a real masterpiece of wood-working art, thanks to its harmonious structure and elegant decorations.

Balia hall: Naval Battle between the Venetians and the Imperial Forces

This hall, divided into two sections by an arch, is so called after the College of the Judges of "Balia" (power), which used to hold its meetings in this very place. It is full of frescoes. The vaults, up to the cornices, were frescoed in 1407-1408 by the Sienese painter Martino di Bartolomeo, who divided the ceiling into triangular sections. In each section there is represented a Virtue. These Virtues are elegant feminine figures, which remind us of the painting of Ambrogio Lorenzetti. It is probably the best work of Martino di Bartolomeo. On the arch crossing the hall there are the figures of the Four Evangelists and six busts of emperors and warriors, while on the pillars there are other minor figures of Virtues. On the walls and lunettes above the arch there is a large cycle of frescoes made in 1408 by Spinello di Luca of Arezzo, called the Aretine (1346-1410). They represent the exploits of the pope Alexander III, belonging to the Sienese Bandinelli family, life and soul of the Lombard League and victor over Frederick Redbeard. This is one of the rare examples of the activity of a non-Sienese painter in Siena. Aretine, however, was well known in the town, because since 1404 he had been called by Sir Caterino di Corsino to paint in the Cathedral. These frescoes represent the last important work of this artist, who was helped by his son Parri, who was twenty at that time. They belong to the long 14th century tradition, dominated by the personality and activity of Giotto.

From the Balia Hall, by a staircase, one can climb up to the large Loggia, open on four pillars, where the remains of Fonte Gaia, made by the Sienese Jacopo della Quercia, are kept.

The two precious partitions of predella representing "St. Bernardine preaching in a field", in the photo above, and "The miraculous deliverance of Genuzia from the devil during the funeral of St. Bernardine", were brought to the Palazzo Pubblico from the Gallery of the Academy during the early 19th century. Now they are in the Pillars Hall which is in front of that of Peace. They were made by Neroccio di Bartolomeo Landi (1447-1500) and probably date back to the artist's young years. We do not know when the predella was made, but we get some indication from the first panel, where the front of the Palazzo Pubblico with the Chapel is represented, without the later additions made by Federeghi in 1468.

Details of the Sala dei Pilastri.

Fonte Gaia, Palazzo Sansedoni

This fountain was built on the opposite side of the Palazzo Pubblico, where once a 14th century fountain was. It was made by Jacopo di Pietro, called "della Quercia", probably after Quercegrossa, his family's place around Siena. This fountain is shaped like a rectangular basin, surrounded, on three sides, by a high parapet. It was made between 1409 and 1419. It looks like a magnificent altar made of white marbles, which anticipates some of the basic features of the Renaissance, with its strict connection between sculpture and architecture and plastic forms. Among the sculptures adorning the fountain in the centre, there is the image of the Madonna, surrounded by the virtues and the Creation of Adam and Adam and Eve driven out of Eden. In 1858 the original reliefs were substituted with reproductions made by Tito Sarocchi and transferred into the Loggia of the Palazzo Pubblico. Palazzo Sansedoni, surmounted by a rhomb-shaped tower, this building, erected in the former part of the 13th century and enlarged in 1399, presents the same basic features of the Palazzo Pubblico.

The Gaia Fountain seen from Torre della Mangia.

The Cathedral

The history of this building is long and complicated. Though it is one of the best known and magnificent cathedrals in Europe, we know little about the period and circumstances of its foundation. The first sure testimony dates back to 1136, when a special deputation of citizens was entrusted with the building of the Cathedral. Then it passed under the administration of the monks of San Galgano's Abbey, till 1314. In 1284 Giovanni Pisano built only the lower part of the facade. In the meantime the building was completed with its three aisles, dome and belfry. During the early 14th century, however, the Sienese, at the height of their prosperity and power, decided to erect a new magnificent building to be added perpendicularly to the south-east side of the cathedral. So the building of the New Cathedral began. Lando di Pietra was first entrusted with the works, then Giovanni d'Agostino. In 1348, however, because of a pestilence and the instability of the building, the works stopped and a few years later the project was put aside. The unsafe parts were demolished, while some of the perimetrical front walls, the left side aisle and the walls of the facade, the so called "facciatone" dominating the town, were left standing. So the building of the old Cathedral went on. In 1382 the apse was completed, the middle aisle was made higher and the upper part of the facade was erected by Giovanni di Cecco. Though various interruptions and time have left their signs on the planning structures and decorations of the Cathedral, this wonderful marble building presents an extraordinary unity, from the rich marble facade, with its splendid mosaics, to the more simple but elegant sides and pointed high tower with white and black strips and a series of mullioned windows. This unity is due to the original and wonderful balance between the Gothic elements, more evident on the outside, and Romanesque elements of the interior. The facade is one of the masterpieces of Italian art. Its lower part, Romanesque, made by Giovanni Pisano, is characterized by three large portals and elegant statues made also by

Pisano, here substituted with copies to prevent them from being damaged, while the originals are kept in the nearby museum. The upper part is in the Gothic style, three-pointed and with very rich decoration.

The upper part of the central portal of the Cathedral, flanked by clustered colonnettes adorned with a beautiful sculptured decoration of classical type comprising acanthus scrolls, putti and animal motifs, the work of Giovanni Pisano. In the architrave is a bas-relief by Tino di Camaino (c. 1285-1337) representing St. Joachim and St. Anne.

The modern bronze door (1958) is the work of the sculptor Enrico Manfrini and represents the glorification of the Virgin by God and by men.

In the upper part of the façade is a large rose window, surrounded by busts of patriarchs and prophets, and with statues of the Virgin (on top) and the four Evangelists (in the corners), all copies of the 14th century originals which are now preserved in the Cathedral Museum. The three triangular pediments are decorated with mosaics by Augusto Castellani (1877); the central one is surmounted by the statue of an angel by Tommaso Redi (1639).

A fine view of the Cathedral.

Bell-Tower and Dome of the Cathedral

The hexagonal shaped dome was built between 1259 and 1264.

It is supported by six pillars. In each of its corners there are big golden statues of Saints, by Ventura Tiparilli and Bastiano di Francesco, resting on columns. Above, some shell-shaped niches change the hexagon into a dodecagon, in which there is a gallery divided by 42 small columns with figures of patriarchs and prophets. The figures were painted in 1481 by Guidoccio Cozzarelli, Benvenuto di Giovanni and Pellegrino di Mariano. Above the gallery are the asymmetrical cap of the dome and the lantern restored in 1891. This hexagonal dome is very suggestive thanks to its perspective effects. Below it, the floor shows, within hexagons and rhombs, many biblical stories attributed to Domenico Beccafumi (1486-1551), the most famous Sienese painter in the 16th century. The stories were remade by Alessandro Franchi.

On the outside, the dome is covered by robust ribs and rests on a drum formed by two orders of galleries. The lower one is enclosed by ogive arches supported by double columns, and the upper one has round arches. When in 1376 the building of the New Cathedral stopped and Giovanni di Cecco began to complete the façade, they wanted to make it higher and more imposing. So the building had to be raised and the lower order of the small porticoes of the dome was completely smothered.

The Cathedral: interior

The Latin cross shaped interior of the Cathedral has three aisles.
It is austere and magnificent at the same time, with its play of light and shade on the marbles covering, with white and black stripes, walls and pillars. Here colour dominates. There is suggestive contrast between the vertical pillars and the horizontal decorative stripes. This gives special prominence to the Sienese picturesque fantasy and refined sense of colour. All along the nave runs a cornice, supported by 172 busts of popes, a work dating back to the 15th-16th century. Below, there are the busts of 36 emperors. Along the side aisles and in the transepts there are splendid chapels, such as that of Our Lady of the Vow in the side transept and that of John the Baptist on the left side. In the elevated presbytery there is the main altar made by Baldassarre Peruzzi (1532). It is surmounted by a big bronze ciborium made by Vecchietta, put here in 1506 in the place of Duccio's "Maestà". The marble floor, with its "graffito"and "tarsia" decorations, is one of the masterpieces kept in this Cathedral. It consists of 56 tables representing biblical stories, sybils, virtues and various stories, made in different periods of time and by using different techniques, from the second half of the 14th century to the middle of the 16th century. Of the more than 40 artists who took part in this work, we should mention Matteo di Giovanni, who made "The Slaughter of the Innocents".

Pulpit by Nicola Pisano

Near the hexagon of the dome there is the greatest masterpiece kept in the Cathedral, namely the Pulpit by Nicola di Maestro Pietro (1220-1284), called Nicola Pisano, since he stayed in that Tuscan town for a long time. Nicola was probably of Pugliese origin. He came into contact with the classical circles of the sculptors and architects of the time of Frederick II. Pisano, however, did not simply imitate the classics, but spontaneously assimilated the best aesthetic elements of the classical world. At the same time, he uses classical lines to express new and different ideas and values. And so, his art breaks with past tradition and begins a new one. The pulpit of Siena, one of the best works of Italian sculpture, is an exceptional expression of this revival and artistic and human greatness of Pisano. It is made of white marble, octagonal, rests on nine columns, of which four have bases with figures of lions and lionesses killing animals, four are without figures, and the middle one surrounded, below, by eight figures of the Arts. The parapet is adorned with seven reliefs representing stories of Christ from His birth to crucifixion and last judgement, and separated by statues of prophets and angels. In the pendentives of the trilobate arches there are other prophets and in the connections statues of virtues. This pulpit, sculptured between 1265 and 1268, was made a few years before the other one, also famous, in the Cathedral of Pisa, though it is stylistically more advanced than the latter. Instead of the aristocratic and detached figures of the pulpit of Pisa, its simple perspective and narrative solemnity, we have here a greater power of expression, a more free and complex plasticity, a more lively and dramatic participation of the characters in their deeds.

In the side photo we see a panel representing "The Nativity" and on the following plate, that of the "Last Judgement of the Good".

Detail of the Pulpit: last Judgement of the Good.

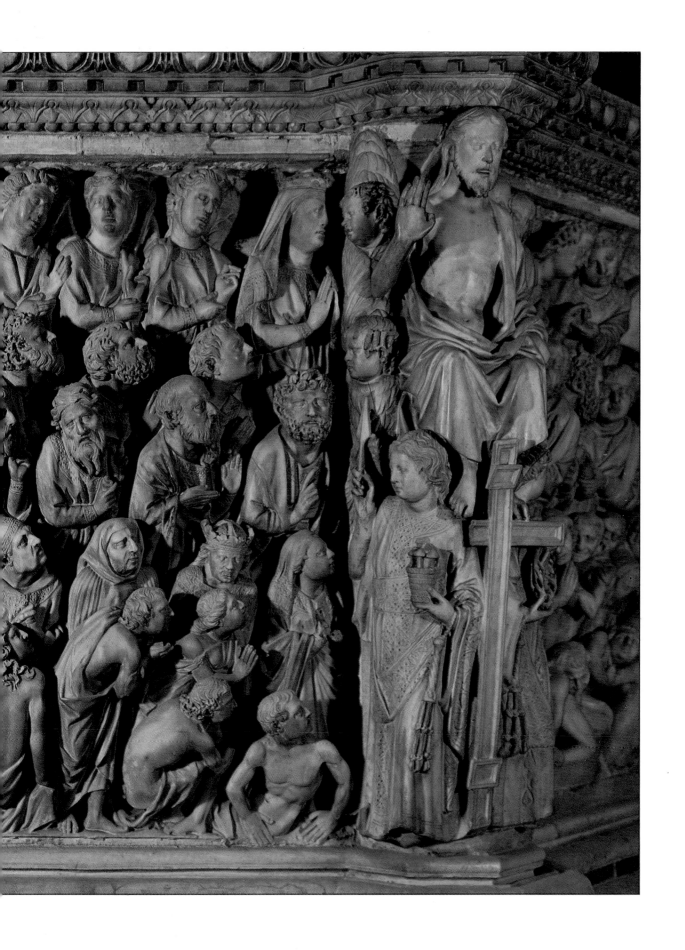

In the photos above, we see the details of the base of the main column of the pulpit, surrounded by eight figures representing the Seven Liberal Arts and Music; below, the details of the "Flight into Egypt" and the "Crucifixion". On the right plate, the wonderful panel of the "Crucifixion", a very realistic and dramatic scene. For the first time in the history of sculpture, Christ is presented by Nicola Pisano as magnificently human, since the sacred history is where human and divine spheres meet.

Detail of the Pulpit: the Crucifixion.

High Altar

The main alta is adorned with the big bronze ciborium made by Vecchietta, and four angels bearing chandeliers, of which two were made by Giovanni di Stefano (1489) and two, together with the half figures of angels, are masterpieces by Francesco di Giorgio Martini (1497-99). On the pillars, on bronze corbels, there are eight angels made by Domenico Beccafumi (1548-1550). The bronze statue of John the Baptist, by Donatello, placed in the chapel of St. John the Baptist. It was made in Florence and sent to Siena in the October of 1457. It expresses a tormented spirituality and a deep asceticism. This statue dates back to the last active years of the Master and was made a little after the Repentant Magdalen of the Baptistery of Florence, which it resembles in its style and spirituality.

High Altar

In the apse is the magnificent wooden choir, which occupies the lower part of the niche for the whole length of the three aisles. It was begun in 1363 and finished in 1397. Originally it consisted of more than 90 stalls in a double line, surmounted by canopies and adorned by tabernacles and statues of Saints. The part on the sides of the niche is all that remains of the wonderful 14th century work with carvings made by Francesco and Jacopo del Tonghio. The splendid marbles on the back of the stalls were made by Fra' Giovanni of Verona. They were made for the choir of St. Benedict's Convent at Porta Tufi and later placed in the choir of the Cathedral in 1503. They reproduce beautiful still lives and sights of towns. The magnificent middle stalls, in the Renaissance style, were carved by Teseo Bartolini of Pienza and Benedetto di Giovanni of Montepulciano, to a design by Riccio, in the second half of the 16th century. The choir, on the whole, is a very refined and magnificent work.

The Chapel of the Madonna del Voto and Piccolomini Altar

Situated in the Cathedral's right transept, the Chapel was designed by Gian Lorenzo Bernini and built for Pope Alexander VII (Fabio Chigi of Siena, 1655-81) in 1661. Elliptical in plan, it has a gilded tambour and dome divided into eight sections by columns below, pilasters in the tambour and ribs in the dome. The Chapel is richly decorated in the baroque style with marbles, bronzes and other embellishments, including the votive painting on the altar from which it takes its name: the "Madonna del Voto", a painting of the school of Guido da Siena dating to the 13th century. The Tabernacle on the altar and the Angels in gilt bronze encircling the icon of the Madonna are the work of Bernini. The first two statues in the niches to the side of the entrance, St. Jerome and St. Mary Magdalen, were also sculpted by Bernini, while those to the side of the altar, St. Catherine of Siena and St. Bernardine, are by Ercole Ferrata and Antonio Raggio, both of them pupils of Bernini. The marble panels between the columns are decorated with magnificent bas-reliefs of scenes from the Life of Mary, sculpted in Rome in 1748. Facing the altar, to the left, is a bronze votive statue of "Gratitude" by Arturo Vigilardi (1918).

The majestic altar, which is along the left aisle, was made by order of Cardinal Francesco Piccolomini in 1481. It is one of Andrea Bregno's works. The Madonna, in the niche above, is attributed to Jacopo della Quercia, while the delicate Madonna and Child, placed in the marble altar-piece is attributed to Paolo di Giovanni Fei (1381). The statues, made by Michelangelo and placed in the niches, are very interesting: St. Paul, St. Peter, St. Gregory and St. Pius. Cardinal Piccolomini had ordered fifteen of them, but the great artist made only four, between 1501 and 1504. These are among the less known works of Michelangelo, though they are of a very high artistic value.

Piccolomini Library

In the first span of the left aisle is the Piccolomini Library. Its building was begun in 1492 by order of Cardinal Francesco Piccolomini Todeschini, the future Pope Pius III, to collect here the books of the library of Pope Pius II, his uncle on his mother's side. The marble front has elegant decorations by Marrina and is surmounted by a fresco by Bernardino di Betto, named Pinturicchio (1454-1513), with the Coronation of Pius III. In the interior of the library, formed by only one rectangular hall, one is struck by its vivid and beautiful colours. In the centre of the hall, on a Renaissance base, there is the group of the "Three Graces" a copy of a Hellenistic original dating back to the III century. This work was donated by Cardinal Piccolomini to be placed in the library. Along the walls, enclosed in pendentives and strips, are the frescoes made by Pinturicchio between 1505 and 1508. They recount episodes in the life of Enea Silvio Piccolomini, born in Corsignano (Pienza) in 1405, archbishop of Siena, then pope from 1458 to 1464, a famous humanist, diplomat and pontiff. This work, however, does not show the freshness and high spirituality of the frescoes in the Baglioni Chapel of Spello or the Borgia Rooms in the Vatican. Yet these stories strike us with their vivid colours, simple and lively narration, without dramatic emphasis, and with the illustrative capacities of Pinturicchio, a magnificent decorator.

Miniated choir-books. In the interior of the library, on benches carved by Antonio Barili in 1496, are the wonderful choir-books miniated by Liberale of Verona (1445ca-1529) and Girolamo of Cremona (first half of the 15th century). It is a very refined work, which represents the best example of the miniature art in 15th century Italy. During the previous centuries miniature had much developed mainly in North Italy, where it had put aside the Byzantine models and followed the great French-Gothic tradition. In the 13th century the miniature production in Bologna and Emilia was remarkable for quality and quantity. These artists were specialized in illustrating civil and canon law books used in the University. And it was the

Bolognese School that influenced the production in central Italy, where it was less rich and interesting, though there were works of great value and originality. Two centuries later, the great masters of the North are still the leaders in the miniature art. And it was in Siena, where they stayed in the second half of the 15th century, that Liberale and Girolamo miniated their masterpieces, namely a series of choir-books for the sacristy of the Cathedral. Today they are kept in the Piccolomini library. Together with the choir-books made by these two masters, educated in the Paduan atmosphere of Mantegna's times, whose stay in the Tuscan town influenced Sienese painting at the end of the 15th century, there

are others made by Sienese artists, such as Sano di Pietro, Pellegrino di Mariano and Guidoccio Cozzarelli.

A work showing one of the 10 scenes from the life of Pius II, who is here holding a gathering in Mantua to promote the Crusade against the Turks.

Cathedral Museum (Museo dell'Opera del Duomo)

The Museum of the Cathedral is situated in the first three arcades of the right aisle of the New Cathedral. It was constituted in 1870 and later renewed many times. It includes mainly works of art created to embellish the Cathedral and later transferred into the Museum to preserve them or because they were removed from their places and replaced with other works during the restorations in the 16th and 17th centuries. The collection includes sculptural and pictorial groups, bronzes, wooden and terracotta objects, gold ware, embroideries and miniatures, all works of great artistic value, thanks to which this is one of the richest and most important museums in Italy. In it one finds some famous masterpieces of Sienese and Tuscan art from the 13th to the 14th century, made by Simon Martini, Pietro Lorenzetti and Jacopo della Quercia, apart from the statues made by Giovanni Pisano for the facade of the Cathedral and the "Maestà" by Duccio di Buoninsegna, all works of incomparable beauty, which are the pride of Siena and some of the greatest artistic expressions in the whole world. On the ground floor, in a hall divided into two sections by a large wrought iron railing dating back to the 14th century, there are, among many other works, fragments of architectonic elements and sculptures of the façade and the interior of the Cathedral; marble plutei of Pisano's school; a front of a Roman sarcophagus dating back to the imperial age; a splendid high-relief dating back to the late maturity of Jacopo della Quercia. Along the walls there are the ten statues sculptured by Giovanni Pisano and removed from the facade of the Cathedral since the second half of the last century. On

The Museum's collection of sculptures.

the first floor there is Duccio's Hall, so called because there is the magnificent and famous "Maestà". Here we can admire also the "Nativity of the Virgin" by Pietro Lorenzetti and the "Madonna of Crevole", a work of the young Duccio, from St. Cecily's church at Crevole. On the second floor is the Treasure Hall, where the most precious sacred furniture of the Cathedral is kept, among which a reliquary of the head of St. Galgano (13th century), a small wooden crucifix by Giovanni Pisano and the wooden busts of the Saints Crescentius, Savinus and Victor, made by Francesco di Vandambrino (1409). On the last floor,

In this page we show two rooms of the Museum, where beside sculptural groups and paintings, there are also objects in bronze, wood, terracotta, gilded work, lace and miniatures.

This is the big lower hall of the Museum, where works attributed to Giovanni Pisano and Jacopo della Quercia are assembled. There are also original fragments from the paving of the Duomo; at the entrance, beyond the gate, is the wolf with the twin, boys, the symbol of Siena - the original of the carvin that can be seen on the column beside the Duomo (which is also the work of Pisano).

The lower hall of the Museum.

Giovanni Pisano: Mary of Moses, Moses, Abacuc, Sibyl e Isaiah

These graceful figures, with their spiral drapery and the brusque movement of their heads, show an extraordinary vitality, which overcomes matter and expresses itself mainly in the faces with their well-defined features. Here we find the whole world of Pisano - a dramatic and, at times, tormented world, where he combines plastic forms with feelings on a plane we could call expressionistic. Placing himself between the classicism of his father's art and the Gothic of the transalpine and especially French art, he reaches the height of his poetic search, trying to create an impetuous and dramatic vision.

MARY OF MOSES, it is perhaps the most beautiful of the ten statues made for the façade of the Cathedral by Giovanni Pisano, born between 1240 and 1245 and educated in the shadow of his father's art. However, he went his own way, rejecting the Hellenic serenity of Nicola and preferring the transalpine Gothic sculpture to it.

Moses

Isaiah

Sibyl

ABACUC, these statues, including the pathetic Abacuc, were made between 1285 and 1296. They represent biblical figures, ancient philosophers and prophets, taller than usual. They constitute one of the most important and daring works of Gothic and European sculptural art and Giovanni Pisano's masterpiece.

there is a picture-gallery and the so called "Saloncino del Conversari", with works by Ambrogio Lorenzetti, Matteo di Giovanni, Sodoma, Domenico Beccafumi. Through a small door of this hall, a few steps lead to the top of the "Facciatone", from where one can enjoy a wonderful view.

In the centre of the hall, on the ground floor, there is, as we have said, the high-relief made by Jacopo della Quercia, representing "The Madonna and Child, St. Anthony the Abbot and Cardinal Antonio Casini kneeling». This work, once lost and recently found, dates back to the last period of Jacopo's activity. It is plastically powerful and deeply moral and this fact shows how the artist, in his sculptures, at times resembles Donatello. If, on the one hand, the rich drapery and a subtle psychologism still connect Jacopo della Quercia with the traditional culture, on the other, the presence of drama, seen as history of which man is the protagonist, is a sign of his participation in a consciously humanistic atmosphere.

The Maestà (Duccio di Buoninsegna)

The magnificent "Maestà" is praised by the chroniclers of that time, who describe the parade in which this work was taken into the church by the people and local authorities. It is the masterpiece of Duccio di Buoninsegna (1278-1318), the first great Sienese artist, who knew how to change various elements into poetic themes by combining the aulic preciosity of Byzantine patterns with the human lyricism of the French Gothic style. With the "Maestà" the 13th century pictorical experience comes to an end and a new age begins. The great development of the 14th century Sienese school is mainly due to him. The monumental painting, ordered on October 9, 1308 and completed after about three years, was supposed to adorn the main altar of the Cathedral, where it was placed on June 9, 1311, but it was removed two centuries later. Then it was dismembered and transferred in 1876 into the Museum of the Cathedral. On its front is the Madonna and Child among worshipping angels and saints. On the back, in front of the "Maestà", divided into 26 parts, are represented episodes of the Passion of Christ, separated by a large middle strip which marks a break between the first scenes, in the lower order, and the last ones, in the upper order. Once this work had a predella with Stories of Christ's Childhood (seven on the front) and His Public Life (ten on the back), and a Gothic gable including 16 panels with episodes in the Life of the Madonna (on the front) and the Risen Christ (on the back). Out of these latter parts, five panels got lost, while some others are now kept in museums and foreign collections; others, 19 panels, are kept in the Museum together with the front and the back of the work.

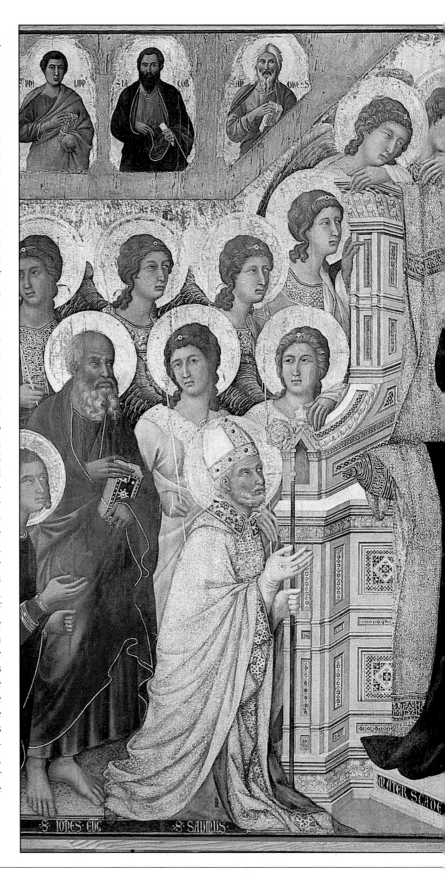

Episodes of the Passion of Christ

Here we can admire the 26 panels of the back, representing the Stories of the Passion of Christ, from the Entry in Jerusalem to the Apparition at Emmaus, where a new and different harmony is created by the play of colours and lines in a constant and various rhythm, including each scene and the scenes of the whole cycle. In the middle, the panel of the Crucifixion, larger than the others, and tragically beautiful. On a golden background, above a crowd of various people, Christ divides the scene in a dramatic crescendo, where Duccio's art reaches the height of poetry.

The 26 panels - From above and from left to right:
1/2 Christ sent to Pilate and Christ before Herod. 3/4 The Scourging and Crowning with Thorns. 5/6 Going up to Calvary and Pilate washing his hands. 7 The Crucifixion. 8/9 Christ taken down from the cross and buried. 10/11 Mary at the Tomb and the Descent into Limbo. 12/13 Apparition at Emmaus and "Noli me tangere" (Do not touch me).
Lower panels:
14 Jesus entering Jerusalem. 15/16 Jesus washing His disciples' feet and the Last Supper. 17/18 Judas' Pact and Christ's Farewell. 19/20 Judas' kiss and Prayer in the Garden. 21/22 Christ before Annah and Peter's Denial. 23/24 Christ beaten and Christ before Caiphah. 25/26 Christ accused by the Pharisees and Christ before Pilate.

The Baptistery

The Baptistery, called also "Pieve di San Giovanni", rises at the back of the Cathedral and is the base of the continuation of its head, like a crypt. Its facade, begun in 1317 and again in 1382, erroneously attributed to Giacomo di Mino del Pelliciaio, was probably made by Domenico d'Agostino. It shows a true decorative preciosity.

Incomplete in its upper part, it is mostly made of white marble and consists of three large portals flanked with small columns and marble decorations. In the middle there are pensile arches and, above, blind ogive windows. On the floor, before the portals, are marble graffiti representing the Sacraments of Baptism and Confirmation; that before the left door, representing the "Birth of Man" with a woman in labour and a newborn baby, is one of the works of Bartolomeo di Mariano, called "Mandriano" (1450). The other two, with the scene of the Baptism before the main door and Confirmation before the right portal, were made by Antonio Federighi (1451). The interior of the Baptistery is vast and luminous. It was completed in 1325 under the direction of Camaino di Crescentino. It is rectangular and divided into three aisles. Its vaults, apse and two

lunettes above the side altars are completely covered with frescoes. Those made by Lorenzo di Pietro, called Vecchietta (1447-1450) are very precious. They occupy the vaults where are represented the Articles of the Creed, the Prophets and the Sybils, and the walls of the apse with two scenes in the life of Christ, the "Scourging" and "Going to Calvary". The other paintings were made by Michele di Matteo of Bologna and Benvenuto di Giovanni (late 15th century).

The reliefs around the small well begin, on the side towards the altar, with "The Angel announcing the Baptist's Birth to Zachariah", by Jacopo della Quercia (1428-29) and go on with the "Baptist's Birth" and the "Baptist's Preaching", by Giovanni di Turino (1427), the "Baptism of Christ" and the "Arrest of the Baptist", by Lorenzo Ghiberti (1427) and "Herod's Banquet" by Donatello (1427). With the six bas-reliefs alternate some statues made by Donatello, "Faith" and "Hope", by Giovanni di Turino, "Justice", "Charity" and "Providence", and by Goro di Ser Neroccio, "Fortitude".

The interior of the Baptistery is rectangular, and is divided into three naves. Both the ceiling and the apse are completely covered with frescoes; in the centre stands the Baptismal Font, a magnificente creation by Jacopo della Quercia.

The statues of prophets adorning the ciborium in the niches, were made by Jacopo della Quercia, while Turino made the delicate Madonna and Child on the door. Donatello and Giovanni di Turino made also the bronze angels on the front of the tabernacle. Many artists took part in the building of the Font. In spite of this, it is stylistically uniform and can be considered a true masterpiece of the plastic and sculptural art.

THE FONT, erected on two steps in the centre of the church, has, at its base, a hexagonal basin and, above, a pillar supporting a hexagonal ciborium. The ciborium, designed by Jacopo della Quercia, is surmounted by a small column on which rests a beautiful statue of the Baptist, made by Jacopo. The small well, made from 1417 on by Sano di Matteo, Nanni di Jacopo of Lucca and Jacopo di Corso of Florence, to a design erroneously attributed to Jacopo della Quercia, has six bas-reliefs in golden bronze, which extol the life of St. John the Baptist. On the plate we see one of the bas-reliefs made by Lorenzetti Ghiberti (1378-1455), who made also the famous "Gates of Heaven" of the Florence Baptistery. Here is represented the "Arrest of the Baptist», a very refined work, very elegant in its forms and serene plasticity.

The Hospital of Santa Maria della Scala

The hospital stands immediately in front of the steps of the Cathedral, and is the oldest hospital in Europe. It was built in the twelfth century, though a local tradition even claims that it dates back to the ninth. The long frontage of the building is decorated in brick and stonework, punctuated by double-arched and other windows.

Inside the building, a museum itinerary has been arranged, leadin through a number of rooms situated close to the main entrance, beyond the "Sala del Pellegrinaio" or Pilgrims' Hall, with its cycle of frescos on the life and history of Santa Maria della Scala, painted in the fifteenth century by Domenico di Bartolo, with the collaboration of other painters, including Vecchietta. The guided visit then leads through other rooms which are less famous, but equally rich and evocative in character, such as the Old Sacristy, which also contains paintings by Vecchietta, the First Chapel of the Relics, with a roundel b Domenico Beccafumi, the Chapel of the Madonna, and the Church of the Santissima Annunziata. The Marcacci, Novaro and Stretta rooms of Santa Maria della Scala today house the Siena Archaeological Museum. The original nucleus of the display includes some important archaeological finds from Siena, both public and private, which were put together in the final years of the last century and the early years of this one. The exhibits come for the most part from the areas around Siena and Chiusi, and in particular from the Bargagli Petrucci di Sarteano Collection, the City Collection of Roman coins and the Archaeological Collection of the Accademia dei Fisiocratici. In 1951-52, the Museum was further enriched by two important private collections, the Chigi Zondadari and the Bonci Casuccini. Attached to the Hospital in the Church of Santa Maria della Scala, built in the thirteenth century, and remodelled in the fifteenth. In the interior a number of works of art are preserved, most notable of which is a fine statue by Vecchietta, figuring "Jesus arising from the tomb": there is also a Renaissance choir and a valuable fifteenth century organ.

The Pinacoteca Nazionale (Picture Gallery)

The National Picture-Gallery of Siena is situated in Palazzo Buonsignori, one of the most elegant late-Gothic buildings of the town. It includes a collection of works which are very important for the knowledge of the Sienese painting art from the end of the 12th century to the first half of the 17th century. Its origin dates back to the 18th century, when the abbot Giuseppe Ciaccheri collected some paintings to donate them to the town of Siena.

Later on, works from various donations, store-rooms, churches, convents, religious and lay associations, which had been suppressed, enriched the collection. It was housed, first, in the Institute of Fine Arts, later, in 1930, in Palazzo Buonsignori, under the State Administration. The Picture Gallery keeps about 700 paintings arranged in 28 halls according to chronological order or various styles.

The greatest masters and less known painters are present here with some of their works. Works which are masterpieces known all over the world, are exhibited together with less important works. All of them, however, contribute to forming an incomparably valuable patrimony and the most peculiar testimony of the painting school of Siena, which was, as Roberto Paribeni said, "the perfect image of a world, a happy and gentle synthesis of the great spiritual riches of Italy". Below is represented the façade of Palazzo Buonsignori, built after 1440 by Giovanni di Guccio Bichi, a very rich Sienese banker, and a few years later sold to the Tegliacci brothers. In 1476 it was bought by the Buonsignori family, whose last descendant donated it to the town to be used as a museum.

The brick façade, with a stone base is one of the last examples of Gothic architecture. Below it has some blind arches, and on the first and second floors there are elegant three-mullioned windows divided by a cornice of pensile arches. Among the merlons of the crowning there are marble panels with stucco heads.

MADONNA OF THE FRANCISCANS - It dates back to around 1300. It is one of the most renowned works of Duccio di Boninsegna. His art, though grounded in the ancient Byzantine tradition, shows a very refined and pathetically human emphasis.

THE SMALL MAESTÀ, on the right side, is another very fine work by Ambrogio Lorenzetti who made it around 1340. It is very important because of its perspective anticipations and great solemnity.

THE ADORATION OF THE MAGI - It is probably the masterpiece of Bartolo di Fredi and was made between 1370 and 1380. It is a very fine work, thanks to its rich details and vivid colours.

CHRIST AT THE PILLAR, by Giovanni Antonio Bazzi, called SODOMA (1477-1549). It is a spiritually and stylistically refined work, which was a part of a greater work made between 1511 and 1514 for the convent of St. Francis in Siena.

POLYPTYC OF ST. DOROTHY, by Ambrogio Lorenzetti. This work, made around 1332, represents the Madonna with the Child, St. Mary Magdalen in the left panel and St. Dorothy in the right one.

THE ADORATION OF THE SHEPHERDS, by Taddeo di Bartolo (1362-1422), dating back to the end of the 14th century. a very sober and genuine work.

A TOWN ON THE SEA, by Ambrogio Lorenzetti. This small painting and the other one on the side page, come from the Archives of the Municipality and probably represent places of the ancient State of Siena. This town on the sea is probably Talamone, a port of the Republic. Thanks to its delicate colours and clear forms, the two paintings constitute some of the finest works kept in the Picture-Gallery. In them reality is transformed into a magically charming atmosphere. They are very interesting not only because of their artistic value, but also because they are the first paintings in European art to represent landscapes.

THE FLIGHT INTO EGYPT, together with two other paintings, THE PRESENTATION OF MARY IN THE TEMPLE and THE CRUCIFIXION, this work is a part of a predella, made in 1436 by Giovanni di Paolo (1399-1482). This artist's poetry goes beyond reality and moves into a trascendent sphere.

CASTLE ON THE BANKS OF A LAKE, by Ambrogio Lorenzetti. Ambrogio is not a disciple of Pietro, his elder brother, but follows Cimabue, Giotto and Simone Martini. He follows these great artists through the minor personalities who constitute the environment of that time. In the case of this fine painting, the artist was probably inspired by a garrison of the Sienese Republic, situated on the lake of Chiusi or on Trasimeno.

THE HOLY FAMILY WITH ST. JOHN AS A CHILD, by Pinturicchio. It dates back to the late years of this artist, who stayed in Siena for a long time to fresco the vaults of the Piccolomini Library. This work, from the Convent of Campansi, shows all the characteristics of the Umbrian painter, who was an elegant and magnificent decorator.

THE MADONNA APPEARS TO CALIXTUS III (1456), by Sano di Pietro (1406-1481). Apart from this painting, this artist's production is largely present in three other halls of the Picture-Gallery.

ST. JEROME IN THE DESERT, it belongs to a triptych made in 1436, whose upper part is now in the Basilica of the Observance near Siena. For a long time it was attributed to Sassetta. Today it is thought to be the work of an artist who painted in a style similar to that of Sassetta and called the "Master of the Observance».

THE ANNUNCIATION, by Ambrogio Lorenzetti. This work is signed and dated 1344. It is the last known work of the great painter. In it we note the particularly well chosen colours, its rich decorations, a new perspective, together with a conscious serenity by which the Mystery is interpreted.

PORTRAIT OF ELISABETH QUEEN OF ENGLAND, attributed to Federico Zuccari (1542-1606). In the same hall there are works by G. B. Moroni, Scarsellino, Bernardo Strozzi and Padovanino, all painters of the 17th and 18th centuries.

THE NATIVITY, by Andrea di Bartolo (1389-1428), a Sienese painter, son of Bartolo di Fredi, whose disciple and co-operator he was. His style, though influenced by his father's, shows a greater freedom as regards composition and chromatic vividness.

MADONNA ON A THRONE, a detail of the Ancona of Carmel, painted by Pietro Lorenzetti in 1328-1329 for the Church of Carmel in Siena. The great ancona dismembered in 1500, included a central panel with the Madonna on a throne, with St. Nicholas of Bari and the Prophet Elijah at her sides, and a predella with five panels, in which are represented the foundation and the first events of the Carmelite Order. The great statuesque plasticity, the severe harmony of the few dominating colours and a dynamic tension of its lines, make of this work one of the masterpieces of the artist's maturity.

MADONNA AND CHILD (a detail), by Matteo di Giovanni (1430-1495), a remarkable work for its pure and simple lines.

THE LAST SUPPER, by Stefano di Giovanni called Sassetta (about 1392-1450). This painting was a part of an ancona made between 1423 and 1426 for the Chapel of the Wool-workers' Guild of Siena. It is the first work by Sassetta, and very important for the history of the Sienese painting art in the 15th century. In it we perceive the influence of Simone Martini and Pietro Lorenzetti, but their styles are re-interpreted in a new and modern manner. Its colour is intensely luminous and transparent.

OUR LADY OF SORROWS, by Ugolino di Nerio, a Sienese painter of the first half of the XIVth century. In his art, he follows Duccio and the Lorenzetti's circle.

THE MYSTICAL MARRIAGE OF ST. CATHERINE OF ALEXANDRIA, by Michelino of Besozzo (of whom we have information from 1388 to 1442). This painter was very important as far as the international painting art in Lombardy is concerned.
The painting here exhibited is a particular example of his over-refined decorative art.

THE NATIVITY OF JESUS by Pietro di Domenico (1457-1503). Delicate in inspiration and beautiful in its detail, this is the only signed work by the artist who was very active in the Marche, following in the footsteps of Gentile da Fabriano and the Umbrian painters, especially Pinturicchio.

MADONNA AND CHILD WITH ST. JOHN THE BAPTIST AND ST. ANDREW by Neroccio di Bartolomeo Landi (1447-1500). A painter and sculptor, he was a pupil of Vecchietta, and his works mark the epilogue of the Sienese figurative tradition. More so than in his sculptures, he expressed in his paintings a delicate linear style.

THE ADORATION OF THE MAGI, Taddeo di Bartolo (1362-1422), In the present painting, similar to that of the Adoration of the Shepherds, the artist seems deliberately to emphasize the richness of the details and the vividness of the colours.

POPE HONORIUS APPROVING THE RULE OF THE CARMELITES, one of the predella panels of Pietro Lorenzetti's great altarpiece. In these little painted episodes the artist achieved a kind of magical beauty, and succeeds in raising even the most humble aspects of daily life to the level of poetry.

MADONNA AND CHILD WITH TWO ANGELS, by Guido da Siena, a painter of the mid-13th century. Apart from this painting, other works have been attributed to Guido, including a fine altar-frontal also displayed in the Pinacoteca Nazionale.

Oratory of St. Bernardine

St. Bernardine's Oratory is on the right side of St. Francis' Square, where the basilica of St. Francis rises. This church was built in 1326 on the place of a pre-existing small church and later many times modified. Its interior is very interesting for its architectonic structure and frescoes. The nearby old Convent of St. Francis, recently restored, houses the Faculty of Economic and Banking Sciences of the University.

The Oratory consists of two super-imposed orders, the lower oratory and the upper oratory. It was built in the 15th century on the place where St. Bernardine used to pray. Bernardine was born in Massa Marittima in 1380 and died in L'Aquila in 1444. He devoted himself to humanistic and law studies, till he joined the Franciscan Order, when he was 22. He began his preaching ministry in Genova, and travelled all over Northern and Central Italy. He distinguished himself for his genuineness. Bernardine was a providential reformer for the Franciscan Order and for the Catholic world the promoter of a new spiritual zeal, which influenced the religious and civil life of his times.

In the photo we can admire the interesting upper Oratory, with ceiling and wooden walls stuccoed by Ventura Turapilli in 1496. Among the pillars there are very precious frescoes made by Sodoma, Girolamo del Pacchia and Domenico Beccafumi. "St. Francis of Assisi" by Sodoma, is perhaps the most beatiful of these frescoes. The lower oratory is decorated by 17th century paintings: a "Madonna and Child and SS. Bartholomew and Ansanus" by Andrea del Brescianino is placed near the altar, at whose sides there are two niches with the statues of St. Bernardine and St. Catherine, painted in white, dating back to the 17th century. Near the altar there are some precious works, such as a "Madonna and Child" in painted wood of the school of Jacopo della Quercia, a "Madonna" by Sano di Pietro and a very delicate low-relief made by Giovanni d'Agostino.

Basilica of San Domenico

The imposing basilica of St. Dominic dominates the hill, at whose foot there is Fonte Branda, the most beautiful and famous of the many Sienese fortified fountains. This work, in a severe Gothic style and all in bricks, was begun in 1226 by the Dominicans who built the rectangular nave and the open truss ceiling. Around 1300 they built the crypt which, being so large, is practically a church, so much so that it was called the Lower Church or Church of the Dead because it housed some tombs. It was restored in 1935. It consists of one large room with three aisles and keeps works by Sodoma, Ventura Salimbeni, Sano di Pietro and Turino di Sano. The belfry was built in 1340 and in the 14th century the building of the basilica went on and was completed in 1465. It was severely damaged by fire in 1532 and earthquake in 1779. Later it was restored and today it has its original structure. The Egyptian cross-shaped interior has only one nave and is very simple and imposing. The chapel of St. Catherine, on the right wall, is very interesting. In it there are frescoes made by Sodoma, and considered to be some of his masterpieces, such as "St. Catherine's Ecstasy and Fainting Fit", and the chapel of the vaults, which keeps, near the altar, a painting by Andrea Vanni, representing St. Catherine of Siena, considered to be the only true portrait of Catherine Benincasa. Together with other important works of art, particularly noteworthy are the ciborium and two marble angels near the main altar of the basilica, made by Benedetto da Maiano around 1475, two beautiful paintings by Matteo di Giovanni (1479) and a fresco by Pietro Lorenzetti. From the right side of the façade one gets into the cloister of St. Dominic, built in 1425, almost completely remade in 1951, where some fragments of frescoes made by Lippo Memmi and Andrea Vanni (14th century) have been found.

BASILICA OF ST. DOMINIO, the elegant square belfry made of bricks, quite modified during the 18th century, and the incomplete facade. On its left side there were the niches in which some aristocratic tombs were placed.

Alongside: a view of the interior of the Basilica.

Below: the fresco representing St. Catherine's portrait made by Andrea Vanni, a disciple of hers, and on the right side: "St. Barbara on a throne among angels and SS. Magdalen and Catherine»; in the lunette, "Epiphany», a masterpiece by Matteo di Giovanni, made in 1479. The painting is in the second chapel of the left transept.

ST. CATHERINE'S CHAPEL, near the altar there is a marble tabernacle, made by Giovanni di Stefano in 1466, containing Catherine's head. The chapel was almost completely frescoed by Sodoma, of whom we see on the left side: " The saint interceding for the execution of Niccolò di Tuldo", and on the right: "St. Catherine's fainting fit". They are very valuable paintings specially for the figure of Catherine and the harmony of the group.

"THE SAINT DELIVERING A POSSESSED PERSON", an oil-painting on wall, by Francesco Vanni (1593).

House of Saint Catherine and Sanctuary of St. Catherine

C atherine Benincasa (1347-1480) lived in this house, with its beautiful Renaissance portal in stone and a fine brick loggia. Catherine vigorously expressed the necessity of a deep renewal in the Church. She was canonized by Pius II in 1461 and in 1939 was declared by Pius XII patron saint of Italy. In the 15th century the house of Catherine was transformed into a Sanctuary.

Right and below: the Portico of the Italian Free Cities - double outside loggia, a part of St. Catherine's Sanctuary, built in 1941.

The Palazzo Chigi-Saracini

It was begun in the 12th century and completed in the first half of the 14th century and many times restored during the following centuries. The Chigi Saracini Palace, once Marescotti Palace, is austere and graceful, magnificent and elegant at the same time. It is slightly bent in its front. It is made of stone and bricks with two orders of three-mullioned windows and a stone docked tower. Since 1932 it has been the seat of the Chigian Musical Academy, an important centre for musical specialized studies, which every year, in July, organizes the Sienese musical week. From the dark passage-way leading to the picturesque courtyard, one gets into the palace, which has very beautiful rooms, precious furniture, and interesting music-halls with a collection of ancient musical instruments. Many works of art, some of them very valuable, are kept in it.

The music rooms and collection of ancient instruments stored in the Palazzo Chigi-Saracini are of great interest.

The Accademia Musicale Chigiana

The Accademia Chigiana has such an exceptional importance among Italian musical institutions, both because of its origins and because of what it has represented and still represents in the international life of the musical world, that it is virtually unique. But what strikes us most when we skim through the story of this institution is not just the "Almanac de Gotha" represented by those who have passed through its doors, but the unusual character of the foundation and its lasting impact.

The Academy was founded in 1932 by Count Guido Chigi Saracini, a great nobleman who was a passionate devotee of music - if sometimes wild in his judgments. To him goes the credit for having perceived, in the "Little Italy" of the early years of this century, that opera was not the be-all and end-all of music, but only one glorious part of it. The Accademia Chigiana was first known as a "Master School of Music", and was attended in the early years only by 22 enrolled students (13 Americans, 8 Italians and one German). All the teachers were famous - Fernando Germani taught organ, Claude Gonvierre (and then Casella) the pianoforte, Giulia Varesi Boccabadati the voice, Ada Sassoli Ruata the harp, Arrigo Serato the violin, Arturo Bonucci the 'cello, and Vito Frazzi composition. From then onwards, the increase in students, and in the advanced courses, the exchange between the older and younger generations, and students who themselves became

Above: Count Chigi-Saracini.

maestri and custodians of the remarkable heritage of the Academy, all contributed to making the rooms of the Palazzo Chigi a homme for the best in international music. What certainly strikes us most when we turn over the programmes of classes in the Chigiana is that among the students of the Academy are names which have become world-famous - mentioning only orchestra coonducting and violin classes we have Giulini, Mehta, Barenboim and Abbado; Inbal and Chailly, Accardo and Ughi, among the many who have achieved fame. And as result a new and shining chapter has been opened in the relations between musicology and musical practice, thanks to a mutual enrichment which was no longer the erudite discovery of useless musical sepulchres but a way of making even the great music of the past contemporary. And this would have pleased Count Guido Chigi Saracini, that great Sienese patron.

This square, quiet and not very large, is enclosed on three sides by monumental palaces. On the background there is the front of Salimbeni Palace. It is a 14th century Gothic building, enlarged and restored in 1879 by Giuseppe Partini. It consists of three floors, of which the middle one is adorned with six elegant three-mullioned windows surmounted by ogive arches bearing noble coats-of-arms. This palace is the seat of the oldest Italian credit institution, the "Monte dei Paschi di Siena", founded in 1472. On the right side of the square there is the Renaissance Spannocchi Palace, begun by Giuliano da Maiano in 1470 for Ambrogio Spannocchi, treasurer of Pius II, then completed by Partini in 1880. The ashlar façade presents, below, some rectangular windows and, above, two orders of mullioned windows. In front of it there is Tantucci del Riccio Palace, built in 1548. In the centre of the square there is the monument to the economist Sallustio Bandini, made by Tito Scarocchi in 1882.

The Palazzo Tolomei

It existed already in 1205, but was completely remade after 1267. It is the oldest one of the Sienese private palaces. It is made of stone and presents, on the façade, two orders of rectangular mullioned windows surmounted by ogive arches, in which the trilobes are outlined. The Palace houses now the seat of the Savings Bank of Florence. In front of this palace, there is the church of St. Christopher of Romanesque origin, where the Council of the Republic used to meet before the Palazzo Pubblico was built.

The Walls and Gates of Siena

The mark of the communal Culture, which has been kept intact through the centuries, characterizes even today this town, not only in its monuments, but also in the whole area within the old city-walls. Dark and winding alleys among houses arranged according to a very picturesque order, small sunny squares and narrow passage-ways, courtyards and archivolts connecting very near walls, streets sloping down till they meet in the centre of the town, in the large square of the "Campo", magnificent churches and houses, incomparable testimonies of culture and creative genius - this is the

ST. BARBARA FORT OR MEDICEAN FORTRESS, it was built in 1560 by Cosimo I. It occupies a quadrangular area and has robust towers on each corner. From the bastions, changed into public gardens in 1937, one can enjoy a wonderful view of the town and surrounding hills.

CAMOLLIA GATE, built in the 14th century and re-built in 1604 to designs by Alessandro Casolani. It is situated to the north of the town and bears on the outside front of the arch an inscription welcoming the visitor: COR MAGIS TIBI SEN PANDIT (Siena opens her heart to you more than this gate).

historical centre of Siena, the heart of a noble and gentle town, where all speaks of history and art.

Siena rises on three hills which, limited by the Arbia and Elsa, meet near the Campo (Field), taking so the shape of an upside-down Y. It is divided into three main districts called Terzi or Terzieri: the district of the Town, that of "San Martino" and that of "Camollia". These main districts include some other smaller districts - the 17 "Contrade", each having its own flag, seat and church. All around Siena there are the powerful medieval walls about 7 kilometres long and including the many gates.

OUTER PORT, it consists of a high embattled portal, almost all in stone. It dates back to the 14th century and constituted the advanced fortifications of the town to the north.

THE PORTA ROMANA, this crenellated gateway dates to 1327 and preserves under its arch the only known fresco painting by Sassetta depicting "Glory of Angels playing Musical Instruments". Attributed to Agnolo Ventura (1327), this gate too is fortified by an outer barbican.

THE PORTA OVILE, dating to the 14th century and equipped with an outer barbican. Walled into the latter to the left is a "Madonna and Child", tabernacle and fresco by Sano di Pietro.

THE PORTA PISPINI, this is the ancient city gate of San Viene, to which the tower attributed to Minuccio di Rinaldo was added in 1326. It is decorated by a fresco of "Angels in Glory", the precious remains of a "Nativity" by Sodoma.

The Fonte Branda

It is the most famous one of the many fountains of Siena, already existing in 1081. It was later enlarged by Bellamino and remade in 1246 by Giovanni di Stefano.

Probably it was so called after a nearby house belonging to a certain Brando or Ildebrando, or else after an old Brandi family. It is made of bricks and has on its front three large ogive arches, surmounted by gables and adorned with merlons and four leonine gargolyes with the emblem of Siena in the middle. The fountain is dominated by the apse of the basilica of St. Dominic.

Inside and outside views of the Fonte Branda.

Next page: panoramic view of Siena from the Basilica of San Domenico.

Archivio di Stato and the Tavolette della Biccherna

The State Archives are in the important Piccolomini Palace, the most beautiful building of Siena, begun in 1469 by Pietro Paolo Pirrina, probably to designs by Bernardo Rossellino.

The Archives, constituted in 1775 and placed in 1855 in the same palace, include a large collection of records, which are very important for the knowledge of the political, civil and artistic life of Siena and the whole province. They include parchments, more than 60.000 since the year 736, various laws of the Republic, letters and acts of the financial and judicial administration. The most interesting part of the collection has been arranged in three halls. It includes records concerning events and people mentioned by Dante in his Comedy; imperial credentials and papal bulls, the will of Giovanni Boccaccio, autographs

and letters of famous men and women, artists, and records concerning famous works, such as the "Maestà" by Duccio, the Fonte and the Pulpit by Nicola Pisano. There are also commercial records and records concerning Sienese studies, the Medici, the siege and fall of the town and the Palio. There is also an interesting collection of miniated statutes, such as the so called "Caleffo dell'Assunta" by Niccolò di Ser Sozzo Tegliacci (1334) and the "Statute of Merchandise", miniated by Sano di Pietro in 1472. Very precious from the historical and artistic points of view are the "Tablets of Biccherna", of which we reproduce here ten specimens, with the permission of the Ministry of Culture and the Environment and of the State Archives of Siena. This collection consists of painted tablets used to cover, every six months, the

books of the administrations of "Biccherna" and "Gabella". The magistrates who run the main financial offices of the Republic, changed every six months. At the end of their term they had their coats-of-arms and a sacred or symbolical scene commemorating the most important event of that period, painted in the wooden cover of the books. These tablets dated from 1268 to 1659, were painted by the most renowned masters of that time, such as Ambrogio and Pietro Lorenzetti, Giovanni di Paolo, Vecchietta, Sano di Pietro, Francesco di Giorgio Martini, Neroccio di Bartolomeo Landi, Domenico Beccafumi; just to mention a few. Apart from those of Biccherna, in the Archives there are also other tablets belonging to the books of the Hospital of "Santa Maria della Scala" and various Sienese institutions.

"THE ADMINISTRATION OF JUSTICE", it was made by an unknown author who received 30 "soldi" for his work. It refers to January-June of the year 1237. It was made at the time of Taddeo, Count of Urbino, of Montefeltro, mayor of Siena during the first semester of 1273. In the upper part are painted the coats of arms of the four Purveyors in charge. Enea di Rinaldo Piccolomini was Camarlingo "pro tempore». In the lower part, we see the Mayor condemning a citizen. The administration of Justice was one of the few tasks of the Mayor after the institution in 1252 of the office of Captain of the People.

"THE GOOD GOVERNMENT OF SIENA", by Ambrogio Lorenzetti. July-June 1344 - The Good Government is represented by an austere and dignified figure. The four letters: C(ivitas) S(enarum) C(ivitas) V(irginis), that means "The Town of Siena is the Town of the Virgin», placed at the sides of the head, show the devotion of Siena to the Virgin to whom all the people offered themselves in order to ask her protection during the battle of Montaperti. The coats of arms belong to the Forteguerri, Mignanelli and Ranuccini families, to which belonged the three Executors in charge, mentioned in the inscription.

The Palio of the Contrade di Siena

Though we do not know much about the origins of the Palio of Siena, it is certain that this feast, the most popular and famous one of the town, existed already in 1310, when a document of the General Council of Siena officially instituted the Palio to be run on August 16th in honour of the Blessed Virgin. Originally the Palio which took place in the middle of August was only the crowning of a popular feast, after the battle of Montaperti in 1260, with the victory of the Sienese people over the Florentines, it became ever more important and had a political meaning. In fact, by offering can-

dles, they wished to honour the Madonna, to whom the people of Siena had consecrated themselves, and at the same time to confirm the autonomy and independence of the Free Town. Only in 1656 a second Palio, the "Palio of the Contrade", which takes place on July 2, in honour of the Madonna of Provenzano, was officially approved. The Sienese Contrade (districts) are practically the result of the decline of the central government in the Middle Ages. This situation brought people to rule themselves and join various associations. In the 13th century the Contrade were about 80, but gradually their number

decreased and now they are only 17. Today the Contrade do not have only a representative function and their activity does not end with the Palio. Rather, we can say that in the present feverish world their vitality has a particular significance. Each Sienese is so tied to his contrada that we can say that the individual lives for the community and the community takes care of the individual especially on the most important occasions of his life. The life of the Contrada is very intense for twelve months, but specially during the days of the Palio, when a suggestive feast has to be prepared. As a matter of fact, the Palio

is more than a simple folk show or an historical celebration in costumes. Today as yesterday the Palio is the feast of Siena and its 17 contrade, which fight for the painted silk drape. It is practically a rite, in which Siena since the drawing of lots, four weeks before the race up to the moment when the horses enter the arena for the final crazy race, shows its true face and relives with enthusiasm and nostalgic passion a wonderful dream of a splendid past. The crazy race lasts only a moment and is the most exciting part of the Palio. It is preceded by the picturesque parade, which coming from the courtyard of the Government Palace, in the Cathedral square, enters the Campo, transformed for this occasion into an arena, which is unique of its kind. The Parade, animated by the

The Palio: the historic procession.

splendid costumes and the sound of drums and the surprising flag waving, moves slowly along the track. It is an incomparable commemoration of the life and greatness of the ancient Republic. And Siena could not offer a more suggestive and proper backdrop for it.

Some scenes from the Palio delle Contrade.

The noble art of flag-wiving

The brandisching of the flags is a real art, which comes from the distant past in which the banner was the point of reference for every soldier, and the loss, of it meant defeat. For this reason, knowing how to handle it properly could prevent the enemy from seizing it. In case of danger, the standard bearer was supposed to raise his banner in the air, as high as possible, with the aim of calling his troops together. In the most extreme cases, he would have had to pluck it out of the melee with all his strength. Standard-bearers were prepared for this task in special military schools where, apart, of course, from learning the use of arms, they underwent severe training, both physical and technical. It was almost certainly from this training that the play of the banners took its origin, and the spirit of imitation led the standard-bearers to impose more and more difficult developments on the banner. In relation to this, F.F. Alfieri wrote in 1688: "...the exercise of the banners will always be commended among these, forasmuch as in it the foot is made ready, the waist becomes flexible, the hand acquires strength, and the arm is given free play".

The Terzo di Città

The city of Siena is divided into three "thirds", the Terzo di Città, the Terzo di San Martino and the Terzo di Camollia. The Contrade belonging to the Terzo della Città are those of Aquila, Chiocciola, Onda, Pantera della Selva and Tartuca.

The Noble Contrada of the Aquila

On 16th July 1887, King Umberto of Savoy and Queen Margherita, guests of the city of Siena, were present at the Palio. In commemoration of that visit, the contrada of the Aquila was given a frieze around its symbol with the initials "U.I", together with a great two headed eagle, an imperial crown and a golden sun. The colour of the flag is yellow, bordered by black and blue. Opposite the Church of San Giovanni Battista of the "Tredicini", which is the official Oratory of the Contrada, stands its headquarters, in Via del Casato di Sotto. Here the most ancient Palio still existing in Siena is preserved; it was won by the Aquila contrada in 1719.

The Contrada della Chiocciola (Snail)

Naturally, a snail features prominently in the arms of the Contrada, against a silver background, surrounded by roses and by the royal initials, U and M. The banner is yellow and red, with a pale blue border around it. The church of the Contrada is the seventeenth century one of Ss.Peter and Paul, which once belonged to the nunnery of the Sisters of St Paul. This has been the Oratory of the Chiocciola since 1814, and is also its headquarters, the rooms of which are attached to the Church.

The Contrada of the Capitana dell'Onda (Ruler of the Wave)

The emblem of the Contrada shows a dolphin with the royal crown, swimming on blue waves. This nautical symbol inspired the colours of the present banner, which have been white and pale blue since 1714, when they replaced the original black and white. Near the Arch of San Giuseppe, in Via Giovanni Dupré, the headquarters of the Contrada can be found. Alongside is the little church commissioned by the Gild of the Carpenters in 1522, and dedicated to St Joseph. In 1782, it was granted by Grand Duke Peter Leopold to the Contrada, which then made it its own Oratory.

Contrada of the Pantera (Panther)

On this coat of arms there is a panther rampant, but the U for Umberto of Savoy is also present, and stands out on a silver and red shield.
During the Palio, the streets of the Contrada and the Church of the Carmine, in Pian de'Mantellini, hang out red and blue banners edged with white.
Its headquarters is further along the same street, Via San Quirico.

Contrada della Selva (the woodland)

A rhinoceros at the foot of an oak tree with fine green foliage, a golden sun on a blue field, and the U of Umberto I of Savoy; these make up the emblem of the Contrada della Selva. The colours of its banner are orange, white and green. The Oratory of the Contrada stands in Piazza S.Sebastiano in Vallepiatta, a building in simple Renaissance style. It was handed over to the Selva in 1818 by the Gild of Weavers, whose Church it was previously. The headquarters of the Contrada, too, is to be found in Piazza San Sebastiano.

Contrada della Tartuca (tortoise)

The banner of this Contrada has a yellow and blue background and its arms consist of a tortoise on a golden field, surrounded by daisies (margherite), from the name of Queen Margherita, and the Savoy knots. The area included in the Contrada is the most ancient part of the city. The Oratory of the Contrada was built in 1684 by the citizens of the Contrada themselves. It was dedicated to St Anthony of Padua, and is to be found in Via Tommaso Pendola, where its headquarters and the Contrada Museum are also situated.

District of San Martino

To this district belong the five Contrade of the Civetta, the Leocorno, the Nicchio, Valdimontone, and the Torre.

Priory Contrada of the Civetta (Owl)

The symbol of the Contrada is a crowned owl perched on a green branch. On the red and black background the initials M and U stand out, added in 1887 after the visit of the Savoy monarchs to Siena.
The colours of the Contrada are also red and black. The Oratory was built by the citizens of the Contrada in 1930, in the mediaeval heart of Castellare degli Ugurgieri, and the headquarters are in Via Cecco Angiolici, close to the Oratory.

The Contrada of the Leocorno (horned lion or unicorn)

It is a mythological symbol which distinguishes this Contrada - a unicorn rampant, or horned lion, on a white field with a blue border in which the words "Umberti Regis Gratia", (By grace of King Umberto) can be seen.
The banner is white and orange with blue stripes.
The Oratory of the Contrada   was recently transferred to the Church of San Giovannino della Staffa, situated in Piazzetta Grassi, where the Contrada's headquarters are also to be found.

The Noble Contrada of the Nicchio (Shell)

A large silvered shell which stands out against a pale blue field, a grand-ducal crown, two red coral branches and two roses of Cyprus interwoven with Savoyard knots: this is the elegant symbol of the Contrada del Nicchio. The colours of the contrada are pale blue with yellow and red edging. In 1680, the oratory of the Contrada was built by its citizens, and dedicated to St Gaetano of Thiene. It is situated near Via dei Pispini, where the headquarters are located.

Contrada di Valdimontone

This contrada is generally referred to simply as the Contrada del Montone (Ram), the animal which appears on its coat of arms in rampant position, with crowns and the inevitable initial 'U'.
The colours of the banner are yellow and red, edged with white.
The oratory is the church of the Holy Trinity, beside the new premises of the Contrada headquarters. Both are to be found in Via Valmontone.

Contrada of the Torre (Tower)

The coat of arms of the Contrada is made up of an elephant bearing a tower on its back. After the visit of the king in 1887, the red caparison with the white cross on the elephant's flank was added, and the flag with the silver cross at the peak of the tower. Since the seventeenth century, dark red, white and pale blue have been the colours of the banner, which flies over the fine headquarters building in via Salicotto, and over the Oratory of San Giacomo, property of this contrada now for over four centuries.

Districti of Camollia

The six contrade of Bruco, Drago, Giraffa, Istrice, Lupa and Oca belong to this district.

The Noble Contrada of the Bruco (caterpillar)

The coat of arms of this contrada is a caterpillar on a twig. The creature is wearing a grand-ducal crown, and above it is the Cross of Savoy. The banner is coloured yellow and green, edged with pale blue. The headquarters are in the museum, and the oratory of the Contrada is to be found in Via del Comune.
The oratory was built by the inhabitants of the Contrada in 1680, and was dedicated to the Visitation of Our Lady.

Contrada del Drago (dragon)

The image of a winged and crowned dragon appears on the banner, bearing a small pennant and the initial U. The colours of the flag are red and green, with yellow edging. In 1787, a decree from the Grand Duke assigned the Church of St Catherine to the Contrada del Drago as its Oratory, since it was no longer used by the Convent of the Nuns of "Il Paradiso". Immediately beside the Church are the headquarters of the Contrada Del Drago, in Piazza Matteotti, which was at one time called Piazza Malavolti.

Imperial Contrada of the Giraffe

The emblem of the contrada is a giraffe, held on a leash by a Moor. Above, inscribed on a ribbon, is the motto "Humbertus I dedit". The colours of the Giraffe are white and red, and the headquarters is in Via delle Vergini. The contrada's Oratorio dates from 1824, and is the Church below the Collegiate Church of Santa Maria di Provenzano, where the image of the Madonna of Provenanzo is kept, in whose name the Palio of July is contested. She has been venerated by the members of this contrada since the end of the sixteenth century.

The Contrada of the Istrice (porcupine)

Naturally, the porcupine is the animal to be found on the banner of this contrada. It is crowned and portrayed against a silver field, as well as being surrounded by Cyprus roses and a Savoy knot. There are also red, black and blue arabesques on a white background on the banner of the Porcupine. The headquarters and Oratory of the Contrada are in the heart of the area, in Via Camollia. The Oratory, dedicated to St Bartholemew, is the original Church of Ss.Vincent and Anastasius, which has belonged to the contrada since 1788.

Contrada della Lupa (she-wolf)

The symbols of this contrada are the Roman she-wolf, suckling the twins Romulus and Remus, and standard of Siena. The border of the coat of arms, in white and red, is alternately decorated by small crosses in the same colours. The colours of the Contrada della Lupa are white and black, edged with orange. The Oratory is the sixteenth century church of San Rocco, and this, along with the headquarters of the contrada, is to be found in Via Vallerozzi. It was granted to the Lupa in 1786 by the Confraternity of San Rocco, on the orders of the Grand Duke.

The Noble Contrada of the Oca (Goose)

A white goose with a blue ribbon around its neck appears on the coat of arms. From the ribbon hangs the Cross of Savoy and the royal crown. The banner of the Oca is white and green, edged with red. It was in the "territorio di Fontebranda" that S.Catherine was born, and in the buildings attached to the Sanctuary dedicated to her memory, standing on the site of her house, the headquarters of the Contrada and its Oratory, built in 1465, are to be found.

The Castles and hills of Chianti

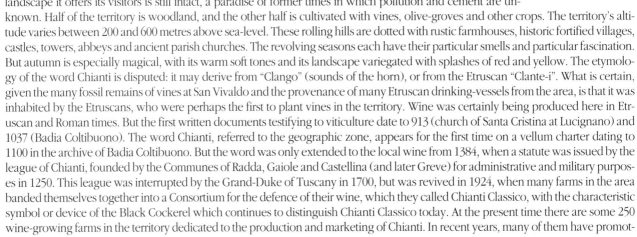

The Chianti area is reached from Siena by way of the Via Chiantigiana. By taking this beautiful panoramic road that dominates the valley, in a few minutes we reach the centre of this territory where the testimonies of history, art and nature which have made it what it is are clearly evident. Not only does the land speak for itself, but the distinctive, brightly-coloured billboards at the side of the roads with the slogan "Siete nel mondo del Gallo Nero" (You're in the world of the Black Cockerel) announce to the tourist that he is in the land of Chianti Classico (for the emblem of the Black Cockerel distinguishes the necks of bottles of that typically Tuscan wine). Situated between the provinces of Siena and Florence, the Chianti territory covers some 70.000 hectares, and has a harmonious, feudal appearance. The landscape it offers its visitors is still intact, a paradise of former times in which pollution and cement are unknown. Half of the territory is woodland, and the other half is cultivated with vines, olive-groves and other crops. The territory's altitude varies between 200 and 600 metres above sea-level. These rolling hills are dotted with rustic farmhouses, historic fortified villages, castles, towers, abbeys and ancient parish churches. The revolving seasons each have their particular smells and particular fascination. But autumn is especially magical, with its warm soft tones and its landscape variegated with splashes of red and yellow. The etymology of the word Chianti is disputed: it may derive from "Clango" (sounds of the horn), or from the Etruscan "Clante-i". What is certain, given the many fossil remains of vines at San Vivaldo and the provenance of many Etruscan drinking-vessels from the area, is that it was inhabited by the Etruscans, who were perhaps the first to plant vines in the territory. Wine was certainly being produced here in Etruscan and Roman times. But the first written documents testifying to viticulture date to 913 (church of Santa Cristina at Lucignano) and 1037 (Badia Coltibuono). The word Chianti, referred to the geographic zone, appears for the first time on a vellum charter dating to 1100 in the archive of Badia Coltibuono. But the word was only extended to the local wine from 1384, when a statute was issued by the league of Chianti, founded by the Communes of Radda, Gaiole and Castellina (and later Greve) for administrative and military purposes in 1250. This league was interrupted by the Grand-Duke of Tuscany in 1700, but was revived in 1924, when many farms in the area banded themselves together into a Consortium for the defence of their wine, which they called Chianti Classico, with the characteristic symbol or device of the Black Cockerel which continues to distinguish Chianti Classico today. At the present time there are some 250 wine-growing farms in the territory dedicated to the production and marketing of Chianti. In recent years, many of them have promot-

ed - as a sideline - tourist development by providing holiday accommodation and other leisure facilities. This land, which represents the heart of Tuscany and its image in the world, was of great importance in Roman times: in fact it was a vital area of communication between Rome and her Empire to the north, thanks to the major thoroughfares of the Via Cassia and the Via Francigena.

In the Middle Ages it was long a bone of contention between Ghibelline (pro-imperial) Siena and Guelph (pro-papal) Florence: its fortified settlements and castles aligned themselves now on the one side, now on the other, according to the military force and strategic positions of the moment. Some noble families threw in their lot with the Florentines (Ricasoli, Guidi, Firidolfi), others with the Sienese (Berardenghi). Of five centuries of war it will suffice to mention the Battle of Montaperti (1260), when the Florentines were routed by the Sienese, causing Dante (in his Inferno) to bemoan "the havoc and the great slaughter which dyed the Arbia red". In 1555 Florence imposed her rule over most of Tuscany, and the end of the internecine strife also signalled a change in architecture: buildings were developed horizontally, defensive towers were abandoned, and the aristocracy began to build build large and magnificent villas for themselves outside the town walls. The first isolated farmhouses also began to appear.

After a period of decline due to the depopulation of the territory, there has been a recovery in the last thirty years with the arrival of new settlers first from England, then from Switzerland, Holland and France, and most recently from Germany, who together with the remaining ancient families have begun a process of regeneration which is still undergoing a period of growth today. This development is especially due to the production of wine, which was proclaimed a "Wine of protected denomination and origin" (i.e. appellation contrôlée) by the Grand-Duke of Tuscany, Pietro Leopoldo, as early as 1716, and is now famous throughout the world. In the mid-18th century the introduction of a new vessel for Chianti, the famous "fiasco" (flask), led to a growth in its consumption and was almost to become a symbol of it. But it was not until 1870 that an official formula for the production of Chianti Classico was issued: this was when Bettino Ricasoli (1808-1890), founder of the modern oenology of Chianti, codified the proper mixture for his wine as follows: 70 percent Sangiovese, the grape which gives body and colour; 20 percent Canalolo, which confers fragrance and softness; and 10 percent Trebbiano and Malvasia, which add a slight touch of acidity and sharpness. At that time, the grapes, after being picked and placed in vats, were pressed for three-to-four days until the dregs had well settled. After a period of rest for about twenty days, the wine was removed from the vats and placed in barrels in which it was subjected to the process known as "governo" or refermentation by adding small quantities of selected grapes previously dried on reed mats. Also worth mentioning is the local "Vinsanto" (sweet white raisin wine).

This is obtained with white grapes (Trebbiano and Malvasia) dried on trellises, made into wine after 3/4 months by pressing them through sieves after having picked them from the bunch to separate them from impurities, and then aged for four years in small barrels (known as "caratelli") placed in airy wine-cellars. Apart from its production of wine, the Chianti country is also distinguished for its production of extra virgin olive oil, which a recent article in the New York Times adjudicated one of the ten best in the world. But to enable the tourist to gain a better knowledge of this small territory of the province of Siena, we will describe below a practical itinerary, starting out from the southern area, and listing the most important localities and monuments, of which we will give a succinct historical and artistic description.

Castelnuovo Berardenga is a small wine-producing centre where once stood the "Castello Nuovo": the castle from which it derives its name, and which was built by the Republic of Siena in 1366. Only a few traces of it now remain, hidden inside the Villa Chigi-Saracini, an imposing building surrounded by a beautiful wooded park.

We are now in the southernmost district of Chianti, and only a part of its territory forms part of the Chianti Classico zone proper. Leaving Castelnuovo Berardegna, we now enter the "world of the Black Cockerel" - homeland of Chianti Classico - and, after passing the first wine-producer on the road (the farm of Felsina), we continue to San Gusmé: entering the Sienese gateway, we immediately have the impression of being in a fortified settlement with narrow streets and a miniature piazza.

Turning back by the way we came, we come to Villa a Sesta: the little town preserves no traces of its historic past. But worth noticing is the Castello di Sestaccia on a nearby hill; its ruins still testify to its grandeur in former times.

In its environs, by taking unmetalled roads, we can visit the 18th century Villa d'Arceno, with a huge park containing an artificial lake; Castel in Villa, former castle of the Villa Guistrigona whose keep still retains its medieval appearance; the Villa la Pagliaia and the vineyards of the Fattoria dei Pagliaresi, descendants of the Counts of Berardenga. Here is visible, to one side of the villa, the ancient 13th century fortified tower.

We also recommend a visit to the Castello di Bossi, whose history is inseparably linked with the Berardenghi family, and which suffered serious damage at the hands of the Florentines led by the rival Ricasoli family. The existing structure dates to the 15th century, but incorporates the 12th century keep. The fortress played a key role at the time of the battle of Montaperti, situated as it is close to the site of the battle. It was later in large part demolished, and the building assumed its present appearance, with the villa built over the glacis of the ancient castle and opening out into a large courtyard, a feature presented by many villas in the area and designed to facilitate the entry and exit of carriages.

From here we continue to San Felice, a fortified medieval settlement expertly restored during the last fifteen years and retaining an aura of great fascination.

Though it has experienced periods of abandonment, it is now enjoying a revival, and the wine-producer that owns it is one of the most up-to-date and best-equipped in the area; a large range of high-quality wines and other produce is on sale. Facing onto the piazza are the Chapel and Manor-House which contains a magnificent wine-press.

Above: an ancient Grapes press preserved in a farm at San Felice.

Left: San Gusmé - panoramic view.

The Castle of Brolio

Not far away, situated on an isolated hill, is Brolio, a name of Lombard origin signifying a wooded place, with the residence of its Lord at the centre. The Castle of Brolio, synonimous with the Ricasoli family, can be visited every day in the year. It is approached through a single entrance, once a drawbridge. It is undoubtedly one of the most famous places in the Chianti area, with a long history and many legends behind it. It even has a resident ghost: a lone baron, the Barone di Ferro, dressed in back, is said to wander on horseback through the Castle's domains on stormy nights.

Of ancient origin (9th century), the Castle stands on an isolated hill to the south of the Chianti area, and commands extensive panoramic views over the surrounding landscape. It was a powerful Florentine bulwark, reconstructed in the 15th century after having been destroyed by the Aragonese in 1478, with the addition of a massive circuit of walls, reinforced at the corners by impregnable bastions.

The Castle always represented a thorn in the flesh of the Sienese Republic. By order of Siena it was completely demolished, but was reconstructed by the Florentines for Piergiovanni Ricasoli and completed in 1553. The building we see today, however, dates largely to the second half of the 19th century; of the ancient medieval structure the earthworks, the keep, the Chapel of San Jacopo, the sentry's covered walks and the cellars. In its vicinity Etruscan remains have also been found.

The Castle is today the site of one of the most important wine-producing centres of the Chianti area, with extensive wine-cellars and Manor House (Palazzo Padronale).

The Castles of Cacchiano, Tornano and Meleto

Before arriving in Gaiole in Chianti, we may stop to visit the Castle of Cacchiano, which seems to have been built over the remains of a Roman settlement and is now completely trans- formed into a villa. Not far away is the Castle of Tornano, of which the majestic tower and an adjacent building, recently restored, remain intact. In the same area, situated on top of a high, partly wooded hill, is the Castle of Meleto, one of the most important fortifications of the medieval League of Chianti.

Its 13th century tower is now incorporated at the centre of the existing building, which it exceeds in height. A stretch of the medieval ramparts is also visible. The two angular towers on the east side were added in c. 1500.

In 1738 part of the Castle was convert- ed into a manor house at the centre of estates famous for the quality of their wine. Here the landscaping of the slopes into terraces and artificial embankments increased substantially in the last century in response to the demands of agronomists and hydraulic experts to adapt the land to cultivation and to facilitate the drainage and stability of the slopes.

Nearby is the settlement of Castagnoli, another fortified hill-top centre: its main nucleus is well-preserved, a typical example of a manorial settlement enclosed by a defensive circuit of walls, though this unfortunately remains intact only in part.

Santa Maria di Spaltenna, the Castle and Barbischio

And so we arrive in Gaiole in Chianti, whose territory is wholly comprised in the Chianti Classico zone. A small forti-

The Church of Santa Maria in Spaltenna.

fied settlement situated on the valley floor of the Massellone torrent (to the west stands the ancient castle, now converted into a hotel, and the 12th century Romanesque parish church of Santa Maria a Spaltenna), it has since time immemorial been a market for the trading of goods, animals and the produce of the land. Its name appears for the first time in a donation to the Badia (abbey) of Poggibonsi in 998. It seems that its first inhabitants came from Barbischio, a

The Castle of Spaltenna.

picturesque fortified settlement situated on top of a wooded hill to the east of Gaiole. Of its fortifications demolished in 1530 little remains; but the 11th century tower of the keep, entirely restored, is still proudly extant. In the environs of Gaiole is Vertine, which is mentioned in the historical sources from 1049 on. Surrounded by a fine circuit of walls, this little fortified settlements comprises many well-preserved 13th century houses, dominated by a massive tower and the keep of the ancient castle.

Continuing our itinerary, we come to

The fortified settlement of Barbischio.

San Donato in Perano. Here we find a 17th century villa which has absorbed the remains of the medieval fortifications. Its tallest part is also its most ancient. The fine 16th century portal of the Chapel may be noted in the façade.

The Abbey of Coltibuono and Pieve Asciata

As the last stage of our itinerary, we ascend to Badia a Coltibuono (600 m.), a complex consisting of an Abbey, a wine-producing farm and a restaurant. It is certain that the friars of the Vallombrosan Order cultivated vines and olives here since 1100. The Abbey, dating to 1049, is a fine example of Romanesque architecture, with a Latin-cross plan and a dome resting on an octagonal base over the crossing. To its left is the bell-tower dating to 1160; to its right the monastery (c.

The Abbey of Coltibuono.

1800) now converted into a residence. Etruscan excavations have been carried out in its vicinity, on the Poggio di Cetamura. Also in the southern part of the Sienese Chianti area we find the village of Pianella, beyond which we once again enter the "World of the Black Cockerel": land of Chianti Classico. A short distance ahead, by making a small detour to the right, we may visit San Giusto a Rentennano. Here we find a Renaissance villa built over the fortress

A panoramic view of Pieve Asciata.

of the Ricasoli, which was destroyed by the Sienese in 1390: it was on that occasion that gunpowder was used for the first time in Tuscany. In its vicinity, a further detour may be recommended to those who like to discover the most hidden and uncontaminated corners of this rural paradise: a visit, namely, to the Canonica of Cerreto, a well-preserved Romanesque church with a single nave and bell-tower. In its vicinity the remains of the Castle of Cerreto can be glimpsed amid dense woodland; only some stretches of wall and the ruins of a tower remain.

We then come to Pieve Asciata, a fortified church with a fine bell-tower. From here we continue to Selvole. Of its ancient castle we can see only some stretches of its bastions and ramparts, as well as an imposing keep which has been restored; though truncated it must once have been a fortification of great importance.

San Polo in Rosso, grape-harvest in the Chianti country

Over the ruins of the Castle was erected the villa of the Malavolti family, a fine example of late 18th century Sienese architecture, with interior decorations of great interest. The ancient Oratory of San

Radda in Chianti: the tower over the southern wall.

Martino, with a 16th century portal, is also of considerable interest.

A short distance further ahead is San Sano. This is a characteristic agricultural centre huddled round the small parish church. The monument to a frog ("Rana Beona") is curious.

We continue to Lecchi where we can see the Castello di Monteluco a Lecchi, which belonged for centuries - like many other castles - to the powerful Ricasoli family. It has recently undergone a ques-

tionable restoration. In the past, in view of its dominant strategic position, it was frequently involved in the wars between Siena and Florence. Worth noting in the same area is the Romanesque church of San Martino.

We now continue in the direction of Radda and soon come to two wonderful sights: the first in Castello di Ama, a stronghold of Etruscan origin which is mentioned for the first time as a hamlet in 998. During the prolonged war between the Sienese and the Florentines, it suffered repeated invasions, causing grave damage to its buildings. Of the ancient castle no trace remains: it was demolished by the Aragonese in the 15th century. Its recovery was slow, and only in the late 17th and early 18th century were the Villa Pianigiani and Villa Riccucci built over the ruins of the castle, completely altering the settlement's appearance. The second notable monument we come to on the road to Radda is one of the most magnificent fortified parish churches in the Chianti country: San Polo in Rosso. It too was the property of the Ricasoli and suffered all the vicissitudes to which the history of the area was subject, including a siege by the Aragonese to whom it surrendered. Returning to Florentine control, its fortifications were reinforced. During the present century, major restorations were carried out by the Ricasoli, including the construction of a balcony over the main façade, and a stone-built ancillary building, used as a farmhouse.

Just before reaching Radda we can make a brief visit to the parish church of San Giusto in Salcio.

Radda in Chianti and Castle of Volpaia

Radda in Chianti, situated on a hilltop at an altitude of 530 m., together with its surrounding territory forms part of the Chianti Classico area. It still retains its medieval town-plan, radiating outwards from its centre: the ancient parish church of San Niccolò around which the town is huddled.

Capital of the League of Chianti since 1415, whose banners bore the heraldic device of the Black Cockerel, which is now the trade-mark of Chianti Classico, Radda in Chianti was the seat of the

podestà (chief magistrate) with jurisdiction over the three districts of Radda, Gaiole and Castellina. Located on the confines of Florentine territory, the Castle of Radda was often involved in the protracted and sometimes bloody hostilities between Florence and its rival Siena: it was damaged for the first time by the Sienese in 1268, and occupied by Charles of Anjou in 1478. All that remains of it today are some stretches of ramparts and the ruins of towers. The 15th century Palazzo del Podestà, seat of the medieval government and now the Town Hall, has an important fresco of the Florentine school in its atrium. Just outside the little town is situated a Franciscan Monastery, built in late-Gothic style, with a 16th century portal. A scenic walk leads under the western walls of the town, from where magnificent views can be enjoyed over the valley and the surrounding hills clad in vineyards and woods. Radda's economy is today mainly based on the production and marketing of wine and incipient tourism. Worth visiting, to the north of Radda, almost on the slopes of Monte Querciabella, is Volpaia on account of its medieval castle. Dating back to the 10th century, the Castle has an elliptical plan, and is still pervaded by a sombre medieval atmosphere. There are many medieval buildings, including the church of Volpaia and especially the Commenda (benefice) of Sant'Eufrosino, which is now used for exhibitions and other cultural events. Below it is a wine-cellar in which the famous wine of the hills of Radda is aged.

The main façade of the Castle of Volpaia.

Villa Vistarenni and the Certosa di Pontignano

Also in the vicinity of Radda is the magnificent 16th century Villa Vistarenni, built by the Strozzi family. The locality is mentioned as early as the 11th century. Also well worthwhile is a visit to "Il Piccolo Museo del Chianti" at Montevertine: a small museum containing a fascinating collection of tools, implements and household objects which vividly conjure up a picture of the area's traditional rural society in the past. Nearby is the National Park of Cavriglia, a delight for children, in which many animals are kept in a state of semi-liberty.

Returning in our tracks, we now take the Vagliagli road, a route that passes close to the springs of the Arbia, through a characteristic and poetic landscape. From here we reach the Villa dell'Aiola, situated over an embankment supported by a system of fortifications surrounded by broad moats. The state of conservation is excellent and gives some indication of what an imposing castle it must have been. Of the four original towers two still remain. These and the surviving ramparts represent, in size and impressiveness, one of the most interesting examples of fortifications in the Chianti area. Before continuing our itinerary beyond Vagliagli, an interesting agricultural settlement, we recommend a visit to the Certosa (charterhouse) of Pontignano. This was founded in 1342, and underwent alterations and enlargements in the 17th century, with the addition of the Large Cloisters. The interior of the church is decorated with fine frescoes, below which are some fine carved and inlaid choir-stalls of the 16th century. Francesco Vanni's Crucifixion over the high altar is striking. Acquired by the University of Siena, the Certosa is now the seat of the Mario Bracci University College (providing accommodation for many students). The characteristic "Feast of the New Moon" is celebrated at Pontignano on the first Sunday in July each year.

View of the façade of the Villa Vistarenni.

Large Cloisters in the Certosa of Pontignano.

Fonterutoli, San Leonino and the Fortress of Castellina

Following the Via Chiantigiana, main highway of the Chianti area, we pass through Querciagrossa, where the great 15th century sculptor Jacopo della Quercia was born; his best known works include the "Fonte Gaia" in the Campo at Siena. We may stop here a moment to see the remains of a castle situated on the left just before leaving the little town.

Before arriving in Castellina in Chianti we come to Fonterutoli, an ancient Etrusco-Roman settlement. A number of Etruscan tombs have been found in its vicinity, while a few traces of paving on the site date to the Roman period. The existing farmhouse on the site has belonged to the same family since 1435, and its present owner, Lapo Mazzei, is currently chairman of the Consortium of the Black Cockerel

(the trade association for the protection of Chianti Classico). Facing onto the little piazza are a church and a number of buildings in brick of great elegance.

We continue along the Via Chiantigiana until we come to the intersection on the left for San Leonino. This ancient fortified settlement is worth a little detour. Its monuments include the ancient parish church of San Leonino in Conio and the Castle which still preserves its medieval appearance. Continuing along the Via Chiantigiana, we continue to climb until we reach Castellina in Chianti (578 m.), one of the highest towns in the area. Situated in a dominant position on top of a hill between the valleys of the Arbia, Elsa and Pesa, it commands sweeping views over a rolling landscape of arable land, olive groves, vineyards and oak woods. In the Middle Ages a feud of the nobles of Trebbio, it later became a fortified village under Florentine rule at the beginning of the 15th century. The Florentines

surrounded it with a circuit of walls, and turned it into one of their main defensive bulwarks against Siena.

Attacked by the Sienese on several occasions, and occupied by them in 1478, Castellina only found peace with the end of the war in 1555. The town still retains part of its defensive system, such as the characteristic covered sentry's walk along the Via delle Volte, with narrow machicolations from which charming views of the landscape can be enjoyed, and the Rocca (fortress), a massive construction with a 14th century tower and 15th century keep which stands at the centre of the town. Restored in 1927, it is now the Town Hall. The origins of the area are of great antiquity: in fact an Etruscan tomb of the 6th century B.C., discovered in 1507, can be seen not far from the town, in the locality of Montecalvario. A stroll along the main street of Castellina is recommended; it is flanked by handsome, well-maintained town-houses built over the remains of older houses.

Especially striking is the 16th century Palazzo Ugolini with a long façade rusticated in its lower storey. Unfortunately the two town-gates are no longer extant; the Florentine one was demolished after the war because of its dangerous condition.

The Farm-house "Rocca delle Macìe"

Worth noting in the environs of Castellina, close to Casalecchi, is one of the oldest Romanesque buildings in the Chianti country: the Badiola or Santa Maria al Colle. It was in this locality that the Castle of Trebbio, demolished by the Sienese army in the 15th century, is thought to have been situated. Continuing our route along the via Chiantigiana, we reach (by a brief detour) Pietrafitta. Its castle was destroyed by the Aragonese and the Sienese during the siege of Castellina. All that remain today are the handsome tower, the walls that enclose the few houses (mainly restored), and the church reconstructed in 1940. Also worth visiting in the vicinity of Castellina in Chianti are the charming village of Ricavo, in the direction of San Donato in Poggio, and S. Agnese, on the road leading down to Poggibonsi. The latter is a Romanesque church already mentioned in documents in 1056, of which only the right wall and part of the bell-tower remain. Returning towards Siena, we now take the road for Castellina Scalo, along which we may visit villa Leccia, where some stretches of wall can still be glimpsed and which must once have marked the site of a fortified settlement.

The dispersed settlement, with the houses in the midst or on the margins of the estates, is a characteristic aspect of the landscape of the Chianti area, at one time largely farmed on a share-cropping system. Yet the functional position of the farm-house did not ignore or disdain the search for a beautiful site, preferably on high ground, surrounded by or preceded by a fine avenue of cypresses. Moreover, the modernization of agriculture has here tended to privilege the most remunerative crops, especially viticulture. Today, indeed, an increasingly frequent sight is that of large specialized vineyards, whose geometrically aligned rows of vines do not disturb the essential harmony of the landscape and harmonize well with the older farms. One model farm that we pass on the road down to Castellina Scalo is that of Rocca della Macìe, a mainly viticultural farm established in a brand-new farm complex faithfully reconstructed on the model of ancient medieval settlements: a typical example of how modernized farming can be practised in full respect for the culture and environment of the Chianti area.

Lilliano, Villa Cerna and Monteriggioni

This is followed by Lilliano with its farm and the parish church of Santa Cristina, of which only the façade with its portal survives of the original Romanesque building, while the handsome bell-tower dates to the 17th century.

Of the ancient castle and the fortified settlement that once stood here, no trace remains. In its vicinity, situated on a small hill surrounded by vineyards, is the Villa Cerna, built over the ancient church of the Santi Donato e Cesareo of which the two bell-towers remain. The villa itself is handsome. On a hill facing it stands the Castello di Rencine, a modest building with a fine garden and an adjacent farm, although a fortress magnificently surrounded by ramparts and towers reportedly once stood on the

site. Leaving the "World of the Black Cockerel", we come (just beyond Castellina Scalo on the road for Siena) to Monteriggioni, a very distinctive medieval fortified settlement erected on top of a small hill. It was built by the Sienese in the early years of the 13th century as a defensive bulwark and surrounded by an imposing circuit of walls (570 m. in circumference), fortified with 14 well-preserved towers. The fascination of Monteriggioni is unique, both from inside, viewed from the piazza where a famous blacksmith - one of the most long-established in Italy - still works today, and from outside, especially by night when the walls are lit up picturesquely by artificial light.

Above: view of San Leonino.
Below: picturesque view of Lilliano, the façade of the Villa Cerna.

For their invaluable cooperation in the production of this pictorial Guide to
the city of Siena, we thank the following: The Accademia Musicale Chigiana.

Photos: Plurigraf Archivies
Stradella, Il Dagherrotipo, Laura Ronchi, Marka, Sie, Scala.

© Copyright
CASA EDITRICE PERSEUS - PLURIGRAF collection
Published and printed by Centro Stampa Editoriale, Sesto Fiorentino, (Fi).